To K[...]

The Stained Glass Heart

You are a treasure.
God has great
plans for you ☺

Maureen Ann Flaherty

Jeremiah 29:11
all the best,
Maureen Ann Flaherty

CR ❤
Cooper &
ROGERS

PUBLISHING
GROUP

Published by

Cooper & Rogers Publishing Group

11523 Palm Brush Trail
Suite 128
Bradenton, Florida 34202

Visit us on the Web at www.cooperandrogers.com.

Book Discussion Facilitators, Bible Study Group Leaders, Educators, Librarians and Individuals, for a free downloadable retreat & book discussion activity guide, visit our website www.cooperandrogers.com.

ISBN: 978-0-9907960-0-8

Reprinted by arrangement with Cooper & Rogers Publishing Group
Printed in the United States of America
September 2014

First Edition

DEDICATION

This book is dedicated to you, my friend. My hope is that it would encourage you to hold on and press on. To know you are deeply treasured and loved. Most importantly, to help you remember that, even in your brokenness, you never walk alone.

The Stained Glass Heart

Maureen Ann Flaherty

FOREWORD

People are like stained-glass windows; they sparkle and shine when the sun is out, but when the darkness sets in, their true beauty is revealed only if there is a light within.

~ Elizabeth Kubler-Ross

One

Thinking about it now, I probably should've asked for help. It was heavy, after all, bearing all that weight on my shoulders.

So maybe that's when it happened? Maybe when I was slumping just a bit ...

The evening sky with all its brilliant sunset colors slid right off my shoulders and smashed to the ground, scattering a mosaic of ragged glass as far as I could see.

My sky had fallen.

Warning signs? Well sure, there were some: overcast days, gloomy dark clouds, and an occasional rumble of thunder. But this? This was definitely not in the forecast! I mean, it wasn't predicted at all.

The moon, on the rise just moments before the crash, now lies stunned amid the chunks of Eastern sky. Noticing my distress, it still musters an encouraging smile like one of those pictures in a book of nursery rhymes.

My eyebrows and shoulders lift simultaneously as I nervously smile back.

The sun, on its way to retire for the day and a bit miffed about the whole situation, resides closer to the West, illuminating the glassy rubble and everything around me in a circle of light. The edge of the light deepens into shadow, which then deepens into a dark expanse that takes over where the sky had been.

Taking a step, I land on a small piece of cotton candy cloud. It sticks to the bottom of my shoe.

You have got to be kidding me.

Breathe.

The sun's companions, its signature sunset streaks of sienna, magenta, amber, purples, and pinks that had burned in excitement moments before, sprawl across the ground. Some streaks are completely pulverized into unrecognizable sandy dunes and sporadic clumps.

I risk another step. Something crackles underfoot.

What was that?

Like all good questions, it brings additional ones.

Did I just break something?

Will the sky return, or is this it?

The questions hang in the emptiness where the horizon had been, making the space seem that much more … empty.

Breathe.

I take a deep breath, which slows the questions and gives room for reason.

The sky isn't really gone … right? Maybe it's like a box of tissues. You use one, and another pops up.

Politely, I look away, in case the sky wants to change in private. But when I turn back to the sky, tears form in frustration … nothing. I quickly wipe the warm water from my eyes.

I want to call for help, but how would I explain this?

They'd probably say I'd brought it on myself.

I'm so alone.

The fiery glow of the sun seems to dim.

Did something just move?

Breathe.

The gentle breeze encourages me to journey on. It must've stirred the birds in the trees, because there is a rush of air current overhead and the flapping of wings. While slowly inhaling, the breeze's kindness, it playfully swirls my hair forward as if daring me to take a step. I look down for better footing.

Maybe that was a mistake.

I catch a glimpse of my fearful reflection in one of the pieces of glass and look away quickly. Scanning the area, I see there is no clear path, just mounds and mounds of broken glass and glittering dunes of crushed colored sand.

If I take a running leap past all of this, will I land on solid ground—or fall off the edge of the world?

A rustling sound comes from somewhere behind

me. I whip around just as a gentleman appears in an opulent white suit backlit by the sun's disheveled rays.

Wow. He's so beautiful!

"Perhaps I may be of assistance." A twinkle in his eye acknowledges this connection. With a combination of rich dark wavy hair, chiseled features, and a warm smile, he instantly captivates me. "I'm Noctis. You know, like Night. My friends call me Nox."

Talk about your "Night" in shining armor.

"Hi, I'm Anna," I reply sheepishly.

"It's not looking good, is it?" he chuckles. "I've seen this kind of thing before. Happens to the best of us."

You mean I'm not the only one this has happened to?

"We can get through it," Nox says. "In fact, I do this kind of stuff all the time. Let's make something to get you out of this mess. It'll come in handy with the rough patches ahead."

"Rough patches?" I inquire, adjusting my posture to compensate for the fact that my voice just cracked.

"No worries," he explains. "I've got just the thing."

What could possibly help with this?

"Let's fashion a chain from your burdens. They're the ultimate building material. May I?" Nox inquires. As I nod, he gently lifts one deep blue piece of worry after another from my shoulder. They each bend easily under his command.

Was that why my sky tumbled down? I've been balancing a load of blues?

But the "why" doesn't matter now. It is what it is. The sky has fallen—there's no escaping it. I hesitate for a moment. Should I let him help? But I can't do this on my own, and Nox is here.

What had previously been so burdensome to carry—failures, disappointments, and uncertainties— now seamlessly are crafted into a chain.

"Like steel," he notes. "They've had time to harden, huh? Each time you dwell on those things, that ol' internal furnace fuses on another layer of blue."

He pulls the beginnings of the chain from end to end, "Now that's what I call quality." My cheeks burn in response.

I must've frequently recalled my past to create such a strong chain of memory.

One end of the chain hits the ground and cracks a shard of sienna-colored sky. Picking up the broken pieces, Nox tosses them into the darkness, dismissing them.

"Nothing good comes from things that are broken."

Two

From a distance, a weathered hand gently captures the discarded sliver of sienna before it hits the ground.

"There's a lot of goodness in this." He stores the shard in a pocket of his tool belt, causing the hanging tools to gently sway in their holster. They're comfortable old gear, each item essential to the craftsman, and they're well-loved, too, with portions of their leather grips worn away and some speckled with rust spots due to working in inclement weather. These tools could soften the hardest edges, build the sturdiest foundation, or mend the most broken constitution.

He is also prepared for the journey with a beloved walking stick and a tin water container that dangles from the edge of the tool belt.

His eyes crinkle as they review the other pieces he'd been gathering as he followed Anna. The pieces contain all the brilliant colors of her world, all that Anna is, could, and would become—a treasure yet to be discovered. Deep laugh lines trace a familiar trail on his face. Artisan picks up his walking stick and hums softly to himself. [1]

Three

"Is everything alright?" I ask Nox, as the tip of his shoe unearths more broken chips of the sunset.

"Yeah, fine. Just checking for something. But no problem, we've got everything we need." He continues to work on the links, then looks up at me.

"How about you? Are you okay?" Nox inquires.

I reply with a half-nod.

"I'm sorry this has been so hard on you. It may be rough up ahead, but you know you can count on me." Parodying a strong man, he flexes his muscles and brings his fists together as he clenches the chain. He throws a growl in for effect.

Laughing, I growl back.

Where would I be without you?

Four

The moon attempts to shimmy closer to Anna but finds it difficult to navigate the current terrain of sand traps. He would much rather be floating amongst the airy sky with its brilliant complete canvas of swirls, light, and awe-inspiring hues. At a barely detectable pace, the moon nixes that original idea, deciding to provide some other form of encouragement.

Beams of light infuse sparkling chunks of burnt orange, blue, and purple. Their reflections dance upon Anna's shoes.

She was always drawn to the moon's radiance, whether as an adult when walking her dog in the evening, or as a little girl dancing in the fields under its beams. But perhaps the laughing-eyed moon's favorite recollection was Anna as a toddler with her little finger pointing towards him during story time. The moon was proud to have served as her night-light.

The moon looks around for his companions, the stars.

Five

"This should do it," Nox says carefully, securing one end of the chain around his waist and handing me the other.

He gives the chain a tug. I fall forward.

"Maybe we could ask someone for more help?" I offer.

"We'll be alright," Nox encourages with a nod of his head and a smile. Mocha-colored waves of hair playfully fall over his eye. His tone turns serious.

"I mean, you don't want people to see what you have done, do you Anna?" he whispers.

A flush of shame burns up any desire to make

future suggestions.

That is the last thing I want.

I quickly look away, pretending something in the distance caught my eye. *Focus, Anna, focus.*

The cold chain digs into my hands, and the constant tugs become annoying. Nox looks back and gives me a "thumbs up." His bright coat seems a bit faded now, layered with dust and dirt.

Six

Nox is acutely aware that he must get Anna to a secure location, especially when he notices more pieces of the broken sky have gone missing, including the sienna shards he'd just tossed aside. And with the breeze kicking up, he knows Artisan must be close behind.

Seven

*B*reathe.

Another breeze tickles my face with a lock of wind-swept hair. A giggle escapes as I tuck the wild strand behind my ear. Releasing the doubts and forgetting the chains that bind me, I am called toward the West. Turning toward the sun, my stride grows stronger with the warmth and hope the light provides.

Nox suddenly blocks my path.

"I lead; you follow," he states. The soft clanking of my chains reiterates his message.

Breathe.

Turning our backs to the light, Nox quickens the pace down a more tumultuous trail farther away from the sun's glow.

How is this helping me? We're descending deeper into the darkness.

I catch myself clenching the chain. My fingers suddenly loosen with the realization of the hold I had on those mistakes.

Nothing so cold and futile could lead to the building of a new sky.

The wind embraces me again. I lift my gaze and see the branches wave in the breeze. I had forgotten all about the trees and the life around me. I whisper a prayer of thanks for them.

Breathe.

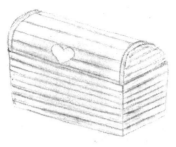

Eight

In another part of the fallen skyscape, Artisan slowly exhales. His breath of life animates Anna's world and stirs the trees.

Artisan considers the options. He loves the concept of possibilities and new beginnings. Some of his best work comes from projects deemed impossible. If the materials are broken or used, it doesn't matter. In fact, these are some of his favorite parts: these precious pieces of glass that contain shiny bits of a person's history, all of the love, loss, and life that created the unique narrative of a soul whose voice would never come again. Whether the story is told in slivers of glass or colorful grains of sand does not matter; the challenge only expands the vision. He will reflect back to Anna all the goodness he sees in her, a goodness Anna had forgotten: the treasure of her soul. He softly sings the song he had been humming all evening:

Shards, slivers, or mounds of sand; none are to be cast aside, for greatness can come from such things.

Artisan knows the darkness will intensify for Anna now that Noctis senses her fear. He has to make his presence more strongly known. Cradling some of the broken pieces of sky in the palm of his hand, he murmurs, "Treasure." Returning them safely to a pocket within his tool belt, Artisan exhales another long, deep breath, summoning the encouraging wind.

Nine

As the branches beckon again to Anna, Nox decides it's time to act. If this situation continues, the whole venture will be a complete waste of time. How can he keep her focused on the chain when the wind keeps reminding her of things he needs her to forget?

Nox knows who's behind all those "calming breezes" and gentle reminders to breathe. Seething, he tallies all those incidents of branches waving to encourage her, and he marks all those missing shards of glass. Yes, Nox is very aware of his rival's ways. The fact that Artisan will invest so much time on one little life is infuriating. Artisan and his light-beckoning trees must be stopped. Whether it is a flicker or a spark, nothing's worse for Nox's plans than light, especially a light renewed.

"I will not lose another one to Artisan," Nox vows.

Ten

"Anna, you need to pick up the pace," Nox says, turning to face me.

The dark circles underneath his eyes catch me off guard. They make his eyes appear hard and sunken.

"With the others, I am usually a lot farther along by now."

With the others ... would it have been easier if I were more like "them"?

I lose my footing again. Searching for smoother ground, I catch another glimpse of the sun.

"And you're breaking too many pieces," Nox warns, kicking another cracked shard into the deepening gloom.

My soul aches. I may doubt the goodness of my world sometimes, but it is quite another thing to see it carelessly kicked aside by another.

"I'm sorry, Nox. Sorry." My voice sounds so high. I try to lower it. "I'm coming."

But the leaning forward and quickening my awkward steps blows my cover.

What am I doing, trying so hard to please him? I hate that.

Looking up, I discover his suit is darker gray and his complexion has become ashen.

Maybe I can try to get through this on my own?

But feelings of inadequacy resurface as my grip loosens and is quickly followed by another misstep.

Suddenly, Nox releases his portion of the chain so I slide down the side of an amber sand dune.

The breeze kicks up, smoothing the marks of the tumble from the dune.

It's wiping my slate clean!

I breathe deeply.

Whoosh, whoosh.

It's the birds in flight again. They sound different somehow; it's like they're in slow motion. Craning my neck, I try to catch a glimpse.

With eyes squinting, my brain desperately tries to register the incongruity of a singular pair of massive black wings circling overhead.

"Stay still, *absolutely still*, and don't make a sound," Nox hisses, enveloping me in darkness.

My heart stops.

"You'll be safe under here." His two wings create a fortress around me and silence the world outside.

I forget to breathe.

Gasping for air, my lungs desperately fill up again.

Stay calm.

I breathe slowly, trying to register what just happened. Was it the severity of Nox's guidance, his strange transformation, or this absolute darkness that scared the breath out of me?

All I know is that I long for light.

The breeze forgotten, I'm pulled into the void, which somehow creeps into my heart … and expands. I want to disappear into nothingness. Minute by minute, my sense of self shrinks as the space I occupy seems to become too large for me. It is as if the whole world is full of spaces, with each person occupying his or her own. And how necessary is *my* little spot in the world when there are so many billions?

If I disappear, would it really matter? Would anyone even notice?

Breathe.

I miss the branches and the wind's comforting touch. It's cold under here. The wind was so freeing; Nox is so suffocating.

Maybe I can call the wind …

Nox warns, "Don't reach out. You'll just get hurt. It's much safer here."

But for me it is a fortress of fears. Each moment another uncertainty enters my soul, while another bit of my freedom flies away. My eyes peek through a small opening between the feathers to see where my freedom has soared to.

I can do this! I just ... need to try harder.

But I'm tired: tired of trying, tired of climbing, tired of carrying, tired of focusing. I miss how the breeze used to stroke my brow and soothe my spirit. I want to hope again.

A stream of doubt trickles down my soul. The sand is shifting, and the ground is slowly sinking under my feet.

Where's the freedom in this?

As a tear hits the ground, I swear no one will treat me like a failure anymore. Nox is company I will keep no longer.[2]

A rush of wind arrives—and turns into a gust. It flaps through the feathery shroud and pushes the trickling stream of tears down my cheek into my ear.

I hop, attempting to joggle the droplet free, and trip in the process, accidently freeing myself from the fortress. Stumbling as I extract myself, I fall to my knees.

Thwarp, thwarp … Nox's feathery talons claw at my face and arms, trying to pull me back in.

I can't get free.

His massive wingspan moves in a rhythmic fashion, providing glimpses of my world and its light as he tries to secure me. Flashes of the sun's light pierce through the feathers, then darkness, the sand dunes, then darkness. There's a break through a lower opening.

Make a run for it!

I bolt across the dunes, but my sprint soon fades as my calves burn and legs wobble. I try to catch my breath. A stabbing pain in my side and a surge of acid in my mouth follows. I cry out into the nothingness: "I can't do it! Please help me!"

A steady stream of warm tears washes away any desire to "try harder."

I just can't.

"Help me!" I cry out, but before the words have left my lips.

"Here I am."

A tall, worn-looking man strides before me. Nox hisses and with one beat of his wings whirls back into darkness.

It takes me a moment to speak.

"Did you just see that?" I say shaking my head in disbelief.

I notice the suede tool belt slung across his khaki pants speckled with small grease stains. "Are you here to fix it?" I look up at him.

A blue jean shirt brings out the warmth of his features. But it's his eyes that catch me off guard. They are like nothing I have seen before. They're so alive, there's an actual *light* that shines about them. His deep laugh lines desperately try to contain joy. He has an old tan coat over one arm.

He chuckles.

"I guess I am a handy man of sorts, more of an artisan really. I do things like rebuilding and restoring beauty."

"I could definitely use that!" I try to laugh but find myself forcing down a burning lump in my throat. "I keep trying to make it better but, it just gets worse. I can't … I keep … "

I stop before tiredness gets the best of me again.

No crying. Just tell him what happened.

Tears threaten to drown my narrative. Maybe by holding back the words, I can hold back the tears. I take a long, deep breath before beginning again. This time my lips move, but no words escape. But Artisan knows, as tears tell the story better than any words ever could.

His voice is soothing, "I heard you, and I am here. There is no need to fight anymore. We can do this." He reaches into his tool belt.

The chain slowly slides to the ground. My hand opens at my side.

"You see this?" Artisan asks, holding up one of the sienna shards I had lost. "Beautiful, isn't it? We can put it all back together, just like a puzzle. You sure have got yourself a beautiful world here. Just needs a little fixing up, is all." He places it gently back into the pocket of his tool belt.

Breathe.

"There is just one thing," Artisan pauses.

I straighten up to prepare myself, although I'm a bit apprehensive. But, somehow my soul feels safe in his presence, and I want to let him know how much I appreciate that.

"Hold on," he says.

"Hold on?" I hesitate. "Okay." I bend down to pick up the chain.

He gently laughs.

"No, not the chain. Promise me you'll hold on and not give up."

Hold on. It seems so little … and so huge at the same time. How can I promise that when I don't know what's ahead? My thoughts turn back to Nox's all-consuming darkness, am I strong enough to journey through that terrain again? I want to believe I can, but all that comes from my heart are doubts.

"Just for now," he encourages. "Hold on just for this moment." Artisan's gaze reflects his belief in me and gives me confidence. His is a gaze of love and certainty like none other—more than I had ever known, more than I had ever believed in myself, more than anyone had ever believed in me. "We'll take on the next moment as it comes."

With that, he gathers my deep blue chain and slings it over his own shoulder to bear the weight.

I will hold on. Hold on just for this moment.

That gift of mercy … so freeing, there is no need to promise more.

My eyes become heavy as peace settles in my heart. Artisan lays his tan coat on a smooth mound of purple sand. Curling up on the soft cloth, the muscles that once insisted I remain strong resign.

Hold on, I think, closing my eyes.

I'll hold on for now and let Artisan do the rest.

I'm learning a new type of strength as I let myself sink into a deep sleep.

Eleven

Hours later, I wake to an unfamiliar noise. Afraid to look, in case it's all just a dream and I'm still trapped under Nox's shroud, I apprehensively lift one eyelid at a time. Relieved, I see Artisan. He is sanding a portion of the chain.

Breathe.

I take in his presence. He glows, seeming to illuminate not only the jeweled pieces on the ground but everything around him. There's no hiding that kind of goodness. His light is too bright for darkness.

"What are you doing?" I ask.

"Lightening up the blue a bit." He extends a portion

of the chain as I near him. "Care to join me? It's the first step to rebuilding your world."

Intrigued, I take hold of both the worries and sanding paper and begin to rub away at the deep blue surface.

He blows on a link. When the indigo dust subsides, I see it has become a light robin's-egg blue. "That should do it. Soon it will be time to let go of this thing."

Free of the chain! To be rid of those blues that have weighed me down!

The thought is exhilarating, but also a bit unnerving.

"Sometimes it's hard to break free," Artisan responds, acknowledging my uncertainty as he gathers his tools. "You've either got a hold of the chain, or it's got a hold of you. Either way, there you are." He crouches down to pick up his coat and begins drawing in the sand.[3]

"Sometimes it seems that the blues are the problem."

His finger creates a circle among the colorful grains.

"But a lot of good can come from the blues. Usually, we don't appreciate that 'til later."

He reaches for the polished chain and places it in

the circle.

"I try to be grateful, give thanks for the situation, even when it's difficult to understand." Artisan winked. "It saves time."

A laugh blurts out. I was definitely beginning to appreciate his sense of humor.

How can he be so powerful and still so human?

Joining him, I curl the last of the chain into the center of the circle. Artisan strikes a match from his tool belt and tosses it in the circle. The carefully sanded links begin to burn.

"Go," he whispers to the chain, breathing into the heap of soft blue and flames.

Paper-thin ash begins to rise and drift. With a gentle wave of his hand, the links twist and turn almost joyfully, bending and folding into a dance of origami, transforming into little blue birds as my disappointments, frailties, and transgressions take flight, each one freed by grace.

The blue birds soar higher and higher, washing away the grayness overhead with their hue, leaving a blue trail of encouragement before fading into nothingness.

The sky is back!

I whisper, "I guess a lot of good *can* come from the blues."

And from such darkness, too.

A breeze nudges the clouds from across the broken terrain toward Artisan. A few are puffy, but most are ragged and bruised. He shepherds them all into a large circle.

"Inch by inch," Artisan shares. "It's a process." Nudging a stray puff back into the circle with his walking stick, he continues, "Inch by inch we grow into what we're created to be. It may take time, but grace waits with you, making sure there is always hope on the other side."

He double checks the area, looking for any last stray puffs that may have wandered off, determined not to lose even one. Under his guidance, the ragged clouds lift off the ground. When they reach shoulder height, they circle around us both, rising and falling like carousel creatures to music—the most beautiful music—that seems to arise from nowhere. I follow the sound and discover that as the clouds heal they shake and release the crystal fragments of broken sky that had injured them. Those pieces fall to more pieces of broken sky below, where they chime sweetly upon contact. At first, I think I must have been too upset to notice the sound when the sky first fell, but then I reconsider.

Only Artisan can take something like a crashing sky and turn it into the most melodic symphony.

My eyes follow the joyous herd of clouds as it moves up towards the blue.

So happy and so puffy!

"If you fall in the process," Artisan adds, "grace will cushion the blow."

It makes me want to bounce from cloud to cloud!

He draws again in the sand, this time a flower bending under a shower of raindrops.

"That's when mercy is at its strongest, when storms roll in." A breeze caresses my brow. "Either it will wash your sky clean or pour down Living Water so you can grow. Inch by inch."

Impishly, I add a smiley face to his flower.

"The best part," he confides, "is that when the storm passes, the grace remains."[4]

With my new world emerging, it now feels safe to ask Artisan a question I had kept hidden in my heart.

The anger and fear I'd been holding burst out of me as I demand, "Where were you? I was lost and frightened." Fatigue always seems to get the best of my self-control.

Registering the loudness of my voice, I try to lower it. "With Nox, the mountains of sand were so intimidating! Darkness blanketed everything … even me."

"Breathe," he reassures me, calmly exhaling with a peace that dispels my distress. "I am with you in it all. And if you need help, all you have to do is ask."

The wind encompasses me. Instantly, I realize Artisan had been with me all along. I want to know more, and as though sensing this he continues. "My love will never leave you behind. At times, the darkness may seem all-consuming, but when those moments arrive, I will send words of love to light your way."

"Words of love?" I ask.

"Words more numerous than these grains of sand."
His hands sift through the tiny grains.[5]

Gazing upon the dunes with a grateful heart, I know
that no one could possibly add up each grain, in even
the smallest dune. The sand is no longer an intimidating
landscape but an awesome and humbling affirmation.

"So next time," Artisan continues, "when pressures
seem too great, give them to me so that together we can
make good from it."[6]

He scoops up another handful of colorful grains,
this time taking a long, deep breath and exhaling into the
sand. He encourages me to do the same.

Breathe.

I breathe out slowly, steadily, releasing the pressures
I'd built up inside. Artisan begins to mold the sand and
warm air, slowly shifting them with a circular motion
until they crystallize. Amazed, I marvel at Artisan's
improvised art of blown glass. Soon he fashions a little

glass star.

Duplicating this effort in a grander fashion, the wind scoops fist-sized balls of sand and swirls each one into a star. "Even when you cannot feel my presence," Artisan adds, "I will pour down an overflowing love."

To create a ladle for this tall order, he sends seven stars to form a design in the heavens, the brightest leading the way to the uppermost part of the sky.

Recognizing it, I laugh.

"It's the Big Dipper."

He looks into my eyes. "In time, when the dark days pass, your kindness will do the same for another."[7]

Seven petite stars take their marching orders and in a final gust of summoned wind form into its perfect counterpart, the Little Dipper.

He continues creating constellation after constellation, an incandescent testament of his love, using a vocabulary so big it could not be confined to a single language, a love so luminous its radiance could not be contained in his heart alone.

The moon, still earthbound, rejoices in the return of his friends to the heavens. It may be out of place, but it definitely is not out of sorts.

I admire how the moon can look beyond its own desire for a one-way ticket back to the sky and celebrate the stars' celestial homecoming.

Perhaps that's why so many children's stories and lovers' songs honor the moon. Like the constellations, the moon reflects Artisan's amiable will, shining no matter the circumstances.

With a burning in my heart, I long to do the same: to extend all the love and mercy that has been shown to me. Courage on the rise, my soul fills up with hope and possibilities.

Please remake me just like you did with the broken parts of my world.

Artisan conjures an image before me. He nods for me to come closer; bravery swells within as I stare intently into a heart imprisoned by deep blue chains.

I gasp in disbelief, "No!"

Simultaneously, the heart expands and causes a link

to snap and fall to the ground. Something loosens deep inside, and in the stillness it comes to me that I am gazing into my own heart. Gauging by the deep midnight hue of the links, I imagine it's been like that for a while.

"I thought I was just loaded down by my blues. I didn't realize that I had sown them into my heart. How did that happen? There are so many!"

"In a rich soil of old wounds, bitterness, and insecurities, the seedlings of pain, regret, and unforgiveness thrive, interlocking one into another. Like brambles imprisoning you," Artisan confirms, "it all depends on what you plant."

I want to free my imprisoned heart. I know Artisan can do it, and he can show me how. The sky's a testament to that. I breathe deeply and push away the negative thoughts bombarding me.

I will learn from this moment and step outside my old ways. I will not close my eyes and wish the pain to disappear. Or worse, try to outrun it; I always wind up in the same place anyway. I will hold on.

The yearning to respond to this call to "hold on" is deeper than any fear.

Taking my new friend's advice, and before going any further, I give thanks.[8]

Breathe.

Then, inhaling deeply, I close my eyes and follow the path of pain that leads directly to the center of my heart. Afraid of what it means—but certain of Artisan's goodness—I turn over that question and the pain to him.

"Although my heart hurts, Artisan, I want to learn from this. Can you reveal to me what this means? I want to be free." My heart twinges as I say the word.

A steady breeze strokes my face. The chains around my heart begin to loosen—a transformation begins.

"Like a tree overtaken by vines or a flower overtaken by weeds and denied light," Artisan explains, "the heart, can be overrun by bitterness and pain, blinding it to its purpose and the treasure inside. You must be getting tired Anna, let's rest for a bit." With the sand and glass removed, we relax on the ground.

Twelve

I breathe in the stillness as my fingers caress the soft blades of grass. I spot a lake ahead on the right. My mind drifts to days when my dog Theo and I would take long walks around our own favorite lake. Off leash, he would zoom by me, then look back panting, with a wide smile and wild eyes. He would roll in the morning's dew for a cool down, then sprawl on the grass as I would rub his head and whisper my own words of love.

I notice Artisan's fingers start to dig at a portion of the grass, pulling up a weed. "Did you ever hear that old adage 'one year of seeding means seven years of weeding?'"

"Nope," I smile.

His eyes twinkle in response. "It means that the seeds of the weeds can remain in the soil for years and when matured those weeds rob the plants of their nutrients, light, air and water, preventing them from growing. Not only that, but those weeds also leave their toxins in the soil."

"Nox works like that, Anna. He delights in sowing seeds that rob you of nourishment. He wants you to become entangled in your past to stay angry and fume over all the folks who've hurt you. Blame them. Tally the cost and want them to pay. Focus on all the mistakes that you've made. He nurtures all those weeds by planting their seeds of frustration, rejection, bitterness, jealousy, and resentment so they spread and choke all the joy out of your life. Sometimes we don't even realize those weeds have been sown into our lives, until they have overtaken us. And you know what his favorite thing to plant is?" Artisan asks.

I shake my head no.

"He likes to plant the 'whys.' Those things that we

will never figure out. The bad things that have happened to us. Why something turned out the way it did. Why some people act the way they do. Those questions circle around and around, ensnaring us and tightening their grip. Not knowing how to deal with the pain, we can sometimes internalize it as the roots grow deeper. We may try to bury it, which only ends up burying us. And no matter how deep you push that seed down, it will eventually sprout."

"So this stuff," the Artisan pulls out a clump of leafy dandelion, "has got to go. And you've got to remove it all. With weeds, even the tiniest bit left can regrow. Remember when we burned your cares until they became ashes and transformed into blue birds that soared and painted your sky? We can do the same with those weeds. When you notice one, pull it up. Chuck it out! Then you can really start nourishing the soil and removing the toxins. Mix in generosity and gratitude to knock out any seeds left behind. The key is to invest in others when you are hurting. Sowing generosity and gratitude will help untangle that grip."

Artisan pulls out a small packet of seeds from his pocket. "Sunflowers are amazing. They pull toxins out of the soil. You can start small. It's actually better to plant a few small patches of seeds at a time than a whole bunch. You may not see a lot of change at the start. But just like a seed underground, there is a lot of growth going on."

"Remember how good it felt to get rid of those chains?" Artisan asks. "What do you say we release those chains of all who have hurt us? The funny thing is that when we release their chains, it frees us."[9]

Free of constraints. Theo races back into my mind, speeding down that long stretch of the lake. Completely content!

I want to be that free. It's time. It's definitely time.

Thirteen

Nox twitches in frustration. Still watching from the edge of the gloom, he paces in the darkness. A committee of black vultures joins him at his feet. Efficient scavengers, they periodically jump up and flap their broad wings as they jockey for position.

Nox's suit is completely decayed; its hue now matches his surroundings.

Artisan has destroyed his chain, link by indigo link; another way has to be found to stop Anna, because if Artisan succeeds and restores her entire world, there will be no stopping her. She will spread Artisan's message of light to everyone.

Fourteen

I carefully pluck out a weed of abandonment, followed by pride. Selfishness gives me a fight and breaks off at the stem. I yank out a clump of lies next, followed with a twinge of regret for hurtful words I've spoken. I pull up weed after weed, collecting them in my hand. The bunch gets bigger and bigger. I dig out one large weed with multiple stems—mistakes I've made and repeated. Suddenly a revelation comes to me. Many of the things I've blamed others for I've done myself. Overwhelmed, I didn't realize I was *doing* some of the things I'd been guilty of. Looking into my heart, the uprooted soil exposes a wound deep and wide.

I hear Nox's voice in my head, "Nothing good comes from things that are broken."

My hand tightens around the bunch of weeds, and they wrap around my wrist like vines. Small thorns scratch and puncture my flesh. As I hear his voice warn, "You will never be made whole. They will always see that woundedness in you." Shame swells. "Hide. Run away, before it drives people away."

Vultures begin to circle in. I can't breathe. How did I slip so far so fast? Tossing and turning on the waves of confusion, I lose my footing. The pressure builds as the storms rumble through my mind and block my vision. My view of Artisan is clouded over by doubts. My heart speeds up as a rush of adrenaline sours to acid in my stomach. Cramping follows. I bend over, struggling to breathe and notice the vultures have landed at my feet. Flashes of all those weeds burst through my mind. The darkness builds. The vortex of Nox's words and my misdeeds pulls me in.

I can't feel Artisan's presence anymore.

"Nothing good comes from things that are broken."
Nox's talons claw away at my insecurities, regrets, and
uncertainties. Anger is cultivated, and I want to lash
out. Seeds of doubt go deeper and deeper. Are the vines
wrapping around me? I'm immobilized.

Shame covers me like a garment. The isolation is
amplified by my comparisons of those who would not have
made these same mistakes. I disappear into a deep grey.

I struggle to swallow. To breathe. The beats of my
heart become louder and faster, reminding me that my
emotions are running the show.

Inside the deepest part of me, a single warm
voice resounds.

Get up.

I stand. I walk a few feet out of my isolation and
declare into the darkness: "Nox! I am not buying your lies
anymore. Artisan has good things planned for me. What
is done is done. I will only move forward."

"I am done. I am done with you telling me how my
life is going to wind up. You don't even know anything

about me. You pretend to care; but in the end it is all about you." I straighten. "I don't want to be measured by your standards anymore. There are no hoops to jump with Artisan. I have wasted too much of my life looking back. I am done. Done regretting, wishing, pretending, and trying to meet the expectations of others. My life is waiting for me. Only I can say what my life will be."

I hadn't done what Artisan said, to toss out the weed after I plucked it out. I held on to it. Then I focused on the bad and not the good. I model Artisan's love and encourage myself to move on. *It is not about falling. It is about standing back up again.*

I begin to repeat the anthem of Artisan's heart: "generosity and gratitude, generosity and gratitude," louder and louder, chasing the fears away.

I search for something I can do for another and spot the moon. It's still shining but looking more like a blue moon. "I know you will return to the heavens again. Stay strong. I love the way you shine. You're one of my favorite things in the evening sky. You're always shining with just a sliver or full big ball of light." I smile a little. "And I love how you play hide and seek between the clouds. One of my favorite things is your super-sized huggable version when you sit just over the sea. They are all the facets of you, all that I love about you." The moon beams back at me. "This circumstance is not who we are. We are going to rise again! You just wait and see."

I breathe deeply and slowly repeat to myself, *"generosity and gratitude, generosity and gratitude."* The clump of dandelions hit the ground.

"I am thankful for you Artisan," I declare. "You're patient." A tender green sprout burst through the ground. Taken back, I smile and continued. "You are kind." The sprout shoots up becoming a tall stalk as I share, "You always are faithful in revealing what is going on in my life, and you always cheer me on in that truth." A beautiful sunflower unfolds. "You always protect me." Sprout after sprout. Stalk after stalk. In time-lapse fashion the flowers unfold. "You always trust." Bloom. "You always hope." Bloom. "You have taught me to persevere no matter the circumstance." Bloom. "You have never failed me." The flowers have all turned thirty degrees. I turn to see what they are facing, and there stands Artisan. [10]

"Take courage Anna. Your faith has healed you. [11] You stood up and you spoke up. It's not whether you have everything together that is a sign of things getting better. It's about the heart and what moves it. That's what makes you a fighter. You are not defined by your wounds. You'll actually serve from those wounds one day. To reach out to another, even when you are hurting—that is what makes you truly strong. Anna, when your body was shaking, heart pounding, and mind swirling, that is when I saw you at your strongest." Artisan states.

My mouth falls open, "Then! When I was falling apart?"

"Then, when everything was slipping away and you decided good could come from that moment."

I don't understand.

"Sometimes when you walk through difficult circumstances, you find your heart becoming more compassionate. You're part of a club that you may not have wanted to join but which can provide understanding. You took a big step from learning to doing. To know something is one thing, but to try to live it everyday is another."

It's his turn to smile, "I've got a feeling nothing is going to keep you down for long. Good can come from brokenness. Give you empathy. You've been there so you can better relate to others."

I wonder what Artisan had been through that made him so compassionate.

He continues, "It is not the wound that defines you. It's what comes out of that wound.

Nox, claws at them so they stay open. I shine my light into them so they become light, like me."[12]

"You see my wounds, but you don't leave me," I say.

"I will never disown you or abandon you,"[13] Artisan replies as he individually plants three small seeds into my heart: *faith, hope,* and *love.*[14]

"Those will be your companions. That is who you are Anna." The lines around his eyes crinkle.

"Brokenness can be good. It can reveal things that are not working in our lives. A lot of beauty can come from broken pieces like stained glass. It depends on your perspective."

He removes the rags of shame and gives me a robe of humility lovingly made in a noble purple and lined in mercy. Delivered with such majesty and grace, it makes me ask, "Who are you, Artisan?"

Fifteen

Before Artisan has a chance to speak, the lake ripples, "You are the Living Water." [15]

And the clouds thunder, "You're the Good Shepherd." [16]

The wind trumpets, "You're the Horn of salvation." [17]

The moon beams, "You're the Light of the world." [18]

And the sun shines, "You're the Morning Star." [19]

The stars salute, "You're the Captain of our salvation." [20]

And the oaks lift their branches and sway, "You're the Righteous One." [21]

While the sunflowers bow, "You're the Seed of

Abraham."[22]

I gather my purple robe and kneel in reverence, "You're him! You're the Prince who rules over heaven and earth."[23] Then I lay down in thanksgiving before him, my face to the ground.

His hand rests on the top of my head, and I look up. "My father heard your cry. He sent me. He knows I understand. I've walked it." He sits on the ground and encourages me to do the same. "He loves his children. You are all precious to him, and he doesn't want to lose even one.[24] Not one, because each one is a treasure. He loves you, Anna. You are not alone. I know you're weary. Next time you're struggling, come to me. When you are tired and carry heavy loads, come to me. I will give you rest. Become my student and learn from me. I am gentle and free of pride. Serving me is easy, and my load is light. We will walk together. I will guide and protect you."[25]

I nod, "Artisan, you *are* my Good Shepherd. You've give me everything I need. You're helping me see the difference between my wants and my needs. So I can really let go, really live. You're teaching me how to rest. To sit in fields of green grass by a lake. You've given me such strength. You guide me in the right paths, and I honor your name. Even though I've been walking through this darkest time, I won't be afraid because you are with me. You protect me against evil. And I don't know how you do it, but you lovingly correct me so I can stay safe. Sometimes it hurts, but I know you do it because you care and you want me to be free. Because you are good, you are faithful and true. You're my friend." [26]

My heart swells as faith, hope, and love take root.

Sixteen

The chains, which once constricted my heart but have now been loosened, fall to the ground. Picking up the strands, he starts to untangle them. "Sometimes you have to face your blues to get to the heart of them."

They become pliable in his hands. Tenderly gathering the links of sorrow, anger, and pride, he elongates some and snaps others into more manageable pieces.

"This is just what we need to finish the sky." His hands continue to work on the former links. "Sometimes when the pain gets too much, we run. Run to addictions or old habits. Try to do anything to distract ourselves to escape. We pretend it's not there or get overly involved in other peoples' lives so we don't have to deal with our own." He holds up an exceptionally bright piece. "We chase after shiny things, hoping it will make us more." He nods and returns to his craftsmanship as he molds another one. "We try to please people to earn their respect. We dive into pleasures to numb the pain and then come up dry. But in the end, it all comes down to the same desire." He looks up from his work and gently smiles. "We all want to know that we are loved."

My upper body sways back a bit, and my eyes peer down, registering what he said.

Artisan gives me an encouraging nod and continues, "Nox wants to feed those insecurities and addictions so that you will be constantly trying to fill a hole. He wants you to buy the lie that you are not enough. That something is wrong with you, that you're not loveable. In reality, he is not trying to have you fill something; he's creating something, a bigger and bigger pit inside of you. And no amount of money, stuff, positions, accomplishments will ever fill it. And that works perfectly for him because as long as you are busy filling that hole, your focus is off of me."

"Anna, what's been your security?" Artisan asks.

I hesitate, my lips suck into my mouth.

"You don't have to be polite. You don't have to protect me or yourself. Remember who I am Anna. I am quick to forgive and want to make you whole. [27] When you share it with me, it removes the power it had on you. It releases the hold. Those sins won't have dominion over you." [28]

I raise my hands, "But I don't know how to let go. To stop doing what I am doing."

"Give them to me." He cups his two hands together and extends them to me. Tears come to my eyes as my hands reach out and the tips of my fingers caress the scars on his palms. I take one of his hands and with both of mine, cradle it against my cheek and gently rock back and forth. *Precious.* I kiss his hand and let it go.

Stepping back, I realize the injury I have caused

him. How I must have grieved his spirit.

"We can break this bondage. When we repent and tell the truth; the truth sets you free. [29] If something causes you to lose your peace, that's a pretty good indicator that it is not from me. When you start questioning, doubting, wanting, run to me instead of it. I can heal the broken hearted. Trust me, Anna. Sins are just like old wounds— they remain open until you deal with them."

I confess, "Before it got dark I felt you calling me, inside, but I ran. I ran even faster, trying to escape. I was even mad at you. The pain and emptiness were overwhelming."

I am afraid to share more. *What's stopping you? Pride? Fear? Fear of what? Of losing control? Of sharing too much because in the past people used it against you? But it's Artisan. I'm safe with him. Maybe it's because when I say it aloud it makes it true, even though it has already happened. Or if I share my secrets with you, you'll turn away. I know you say you won't, but I am still afraid. How can this part of me be loveable?*

"It's not about what you do. It's about who you are,

Anna." He rests a hand on my shoulder. "And you are mine. You don't have to worry about finding me when it gets dark. I will meet you right where you are. [30] It is a come-as-you-are policy. Nothing will ever separate you from my love." [31]

I struggle to contain a sob. *I feel safe. I'm home.*

"Remember how you got up and spoke up to Nox? That's what you have to do every time he tries to push you down. Get up and speak life! Anytime you are immobilized by your past or your sins, think of something we got through together, give me that sin, and press on."

"Artisan, I want to be completely healed. If you are willing, I know you can do it. I am certain that the one who began a good work in me will complete it." [32]

"When you grab hold of those chains of blues or those endless addictions and wants, you're buying into Nox's system of bondage. But that is not who you are Anna. Look at yourself through your father's eyes. I came so that we could be one family. To be reunited again. My dad is your dad. You did not receive a spirit of slavery leading to fear again, but you received the spirit of adoption as a daughter of my father so you can cry out Daddy," said Artisan. [33]

"When you know who you are, those chains won't be able to hold you anymore."

Seventeen

"Now Anna," Artisan smiles, "it's time to remember who you are. Since the day my father formed you in your mother's womb, he has loved you and sung over you."

Artisan gently sways back and forth as he pulls out an old, beat-up ruler and begins to conduct his father's celestial choir. The stars light up across the sky like individual notes on a staff, producing a music box like tune of xylophone and toy piano.

The moon sings in a rich alto voice:

He knows you,

He loves you.

Yes, it's true.
You are precious.
You are treasured.
There is more to you.

The stars join in as the moon's back-up section complete with synchronized moves of marching in place, spins and slides:

On the good days and bad,
His love remains the same,
When you get up or sit down, [34]
He not only knows your name
But how many hairs on your precious head, [35]
He sings over you as you rise and go to bed.

Artisan turns to Anna and sings:
You are his cherished daughter,
truly one of a kind.
Your intricate carved fingerprints,
reflect this grand design.

The clouds rumble in and croon:

Nox is jealous of that love,
and wants you to fail
As he weaves and winds you down
that tumultuous trail;
trying to steal your sense of self and identity
He wants to rob you of your security.

The moon and stars back up the clouds:

He knows you,
He loves you.
Yes, it's true.
You are precious.
You are treasured.
There is more to you.

The oak branches sway as Artisan sings:

So celebrate Anna!
Stand tall.
You stood up to him,

and spoke life into his darkness.
You are the daughter of the King. [36]
Now, you're a deeply- rooted oak,
noble and firm,
but also flexible in the breeze
to weather the many storms and torrents
knowing your father's love and inheritance
has equipped you for this moment.

My heart burns in excitement, and I start to sing:
So I'll stand tall,
I'll stand true,
I'm afraid my life, and shoulders, have been a bit
askew
under the misconception that I'm a frail flower,
but I am an oak of righteousness,
a voice needed for this hour
To hold on,
to not give up
and to forever proclaim,

Our Father's love,
to all his children,
again and again. [37]

Eighteen

"Great." Nox paces back and forth. "She found her own voice. Unbelievable."

"So you wanna play Artisan? Okay, let's play." Nox's right foot begins tapping and with his head shaking he warns, "You are so proud of her. You think that means that she can defend herself now. Well, here's some news. She is not as strong as you think. One little crack in that foundation, and down she'll go. Down, down, down. Then you'll hear her all right."

Nineteen

A sudden breeze stirs the trees. The leaves briskly flap against each other. It sounds like the ocean surf.

Breathe.

His love is overwhelming. Warm tears form, and I begin to weep. "Artisan I am so sorry. For those things I knew that I was doing wrong and also all that you have tenderly revealed. I didn't realize I had such anger and unforgiveness in my heart." [38]

"Don't you know, Anna, that I have been there with you through it all? I have saved each tear that you have shed." Artisan reaches into his tool belt and pulls out a small, green glass bottle with a cork top. "Collected each one, none are ever wasted." [39] He takes the lid off the bottle.

A current of salt air rushes in as a wave of mercy comes over me, pulling the remaining toxins and offenses out to sea. [40]

"All is forgiven," Artisan says.

Collected drops of compassion have become a wave of forgiveness. My sins are completely gone, washed out to sea to be remembered no more.

I take off my opulent purple robe and place it at my savior's feet. "Your will be done, Artisan. Teach me. I will forgive. I will love. I will let go. Day by day. I will walk it. Reign in my heart." A simple kiss on each foot expresses my thanksgiving.

He tenderly lifts my head. "I know you haven't always felt safe. And when those moments return or new ones arise, let my love enfold you like a blanket, creating a hedge of protection." He picks up the rich purple robe as I stand. "You know, I think that I'll write that down so you won't forget it." He smiles. A violent wind storm barrels in, attempting to blow the robe out of Artisan's arms. Still, he calmly directs the robe to rise as the gust dies down. The top of the rich velour garment twirls into a point while the end is fanned out. With a simple nod of Artisan's head, the robe propels towards the sky. "Protection is important. Be wary of folks who try to tear you down. Just like weeds, the wrong choices in company can rob you of your identity. Stand tall. You are a daughter of the King." The tip of the robe writes in purple across the lower horizon: *Princess.* [41] "Remember that you are deeply loved." The robe continues and writes *Precious.*[42] "Remember that you are here for a specific reason, to tell a unique story." In bolder font, the robe adds *Purpose.* [43] "And most importantly, remember that when the storms blow in, I will provide … "

"Protection,"[44] I say as the scribe completes his thought.

The garment flips and with the fanned out portion paints large brush strokes of purple across the lower horizon, transforming the former words into purple sunset streaks and blanketing the sky with Artisan's promises. The robe dissipates into the streaks.

The tempest blows again.

Artisan nods toward the edge of the gloom, signaling Nox's presence.

"Oh no," I sharply inhale.

I take the vultures as Nox's show of confidence, but it's what Artisan says next that totally disarms me.

"There is another thing that darkness can't stand: forgiveness." [45]

Bowing my head and avoiding the temptation to look over at Nox, I thank Artisan for teaching me to forgive all those who had hurt me and asked for forgiveness for all those I had hurt. Then I take a deep breath, and do what is more difficult: forgive myself.

"Forgiveness is a process. It might take some time," Artisan offers, "but we'll get there inch by inch." His loving gaze confirms, "It also means letting go of injuries, events, sorrows, and illnesses that have occurred through no fault of our own, and that we may never comprehend.

But in those moments, there can be a peace that passes all understanding. I'll help you carry on.[46] I'll send you a love letter.[47] Just before the sun sets, the sky will become twice as bright, casting a golden hue and reminding you to let go, because every day will bring a new beginning."

Artisan stands behind me for support. With new confidence, I turn back toward the night.

My heart races, thinking about the grip my former guide had on me. I can hardly believe how quickly those old feelings of inadequacy and uncertainty can return just by glimpsing back into the darkness.

The wind enfolds me, and I cling to the image of forgiveness melting the chains that once bound my heart.

Who would have thought walking through the darkness and pain instead of running from it would lead to such freedom? Nox has nothing to make chains from, no dark paths to lead me down. You can do this.

With my heart pounding, in a low and certain voice, I command Nox to: "Go."

He vanishes. Artisan's gift of light and the freedom

of forgiveness have defeated the darkness.

I spin back around wanting to celebrate with Artisan.

"I knew you could do it," he said. Affirming what was before him, he calls me: "*Treasure.*"

Twenty

"They were right. All this time. The vultures were right," I told Artisan in disbelief. "I thought they were there because of Nox. You know, some ominous sign of things to come, but in the end they were there for me. They were waiting for me to die to my old ways, end those patterns. Standing there thinking, 'it's over—call it.' They *are* excellent scavengers. And their gut instincts were right—not because of what Nox had planned for me but what you had planned for me. You knew all along that I had to die to myself, to yank out all those old weeds, so I could really be free. I want to get better at that. To learn how to put others before myself, to listen more than I speak, and to be open to letting your will be done in my life versus holding tightly to my own plans. How do you do it Artisan?" I ask in wonder. "Not only do you help me bear this weight but you always manage to bring some good out of it."

I bow my head and give thanks for the vultures and for the darkness. Chuckling, I look up at Artisan and say, "I'll never view those birds the same way again."

He laughs, then noticing a passing butterfly, nods toward it, "That's just like you, Anna," Artisan says. "The weight of her wings is technically more than she can bear. But not only does she manage to carry the weight, but because of it, she dances joyfully through the air."

My heart flutters with joy.

Twenty-One

"Perfect," Artisan murmurs, as he returns to his project, prying open a broken link and stretching it into a long, thin strand. He bends it into the shape of a heart.

Artisan then retrieves a piece of sienna glass from his tool belt. He gently molds a fine border of midnight blue around it and does the same with other small chunks of sky he has collected. Each broken piece is set inside the heart until it's filled with the magentas, ambers, burnt oranges, and siennas of a glowing sunset.

"Once you get to the heart of it, it's a whole new world."

He places the finished heart in my hands and

instructs me to hold it at eye level and adds with a wink, "What do you say we get a little light on the subject?"

Motioning the moon to prepare for lift-off, Artisan gestures skyward. The moon lands among the clouds and stars. The luminous moonlight permeates the heart's colored glass, showering me in radiance.

"Instead of allowing the darkness to overcome us, we will overcome it with light," Artisan explains.[48]

Twenty-Two

In that moment, I completely surrender to Artisan's loving care, revealing any remaining struggles and pains beyond reason or understanding. They melt away. Pride scatters and turns to ash as hope blows in.

"Most importantly Anna, don't be mad at yourself for past transgressions. My father's not mad at you. When those feelings rush in, remind yourself that 'all is forgiven.' And know, as far as the East is from the West," Artisan motions his right hand across the horizon, "those things are forgotten. They are remembered no more." [49]

He beckons the few remaining pieces of colored glass to rise and find their place in the puzzle to create a rich tapestry of color and light. The sun, free from imprisonment under the rubble, shoots to the western horizon and settles into place.

My sky is more beautiful and brighter than ever. But out of all the wonders I have seen, perhaps the most miraculous is how Artisan has created a new heart in me.[50]

Artisan asks, "Are you ready to continue on your journey?"

I nod. "If you come with me."

"I am with you always," he reminds me. "Next time, when the weight of the world is on you, call on me. You don't have to manage everything all by yourself."[51]

Realizing how much my former disposition had affected my posture, I roll back my shoulders.

He exhales and breathes his Spirit upon me.[52] My soul leaps with joy as iridescent rays of happiness shine forth from my heart and radiate across the sky. From that single small space where I stood, a lavish display of all the colors of my world shoots up into the crafted horizon.

All those things that were once used to repair the

broken sky, the mounds of sand, and the bluebird-painted hue are no longer needed. The gift of the Spirit has not only completely restored my horizon but renewed it, elevating the sky to an undiscovered brilliance. Admiring Artisan's work, my heart actually feels bigger. Rendered speechless by his artistry, I can only mouth, "Thank you."

He smiles. "The Spirit will teach you what you need to know, bringing forth kindness, goodness, faithfulness, humility, and strength of will to your world.[53] Remember to guard your heart; it is the wellspring of life.[54] For where your heart is, that is where your treasure will also be."[55]

I nod.

"Most importantly, remember that nothing can separate you from my love."[56]

Looking into his eyes, I know it is true because with Artisan, anything is possible.[57]

I am ready to begin again; my destiny is before me.

Thanking the moon and stars for their lovely companionship, I tell my friends I will see them again this evening, and then I turn towards the sun. Just like the sunflowers.

I think of Artisan. *That's when I lighten up—when you shine through me. I will remember the love and wisdom Artisan shared, as I take each day moment by moment. Reflecting that love to others, I am empowered knowing that my life, along with all of Artisan's creation, is a treasure.*

I cradle my much-loved stained glass heart. Then standing tall, I breathe and step into the light of a new day.

THERE IS MORE TO THE STORY ...

"O thou afflicted, tossed with tempest, and not comforted, behold, I will set thy stones in fair colors, and lay thou foundation with sapphires."

Isaiah 54:11

American Standard Version (ASV)

The Stained Glass Heart is an allegory,
which is a "work of art in which a deeper meaning
underlies the superficial or literal meaning."
These questions present an encouraging environment to
help you go deeper into that meaning
and your own personal faith journey. Also, to be
reminded of God's unending love for you.

Enjoy the treasure you discover in
The Stained Glass Heart!

The Stained Glass Heart
Your Journey Begins

Chapter One

1. *Warning signs? Well sure, there were some: overcast days, gloomy dark clouds, and an occasional rumble of thunder. But this? This was definitely not in the forecast! I mean, it wasn't predicted at all. (pp. 1-2)*

Sometimes our bodies give us subtle warning signs when life is too much: headaches, tension in our shoulders or backs, exhaustion. When you feel those warning signs coming on, is there something helpful you do? For example, taking a walk outside, carving out some time for prayer or mediation, or taking a bath? What have you found helpful?

Chapter Two

1. *He hums softly to himself. (p. 10)*

New International Reader's Version (NIRV): "The Lord your God is with you. He is mighty enough to save you. He will take great delight in you. The quietness of his love will calm you down. He will sing with joy because of you." Zephaniah 3:17

Artisan sings over the broken pieces of Anna's world, rejoicing in her even when Anna cannot see her own value.

At a youth ministry conference, I heard a speaker say that when his parents are visiting, his mom stays close to the baby monitor just waiting for her granddaughter to wake up. At the baby's first peep, his mom exclaims, "She's awake! She's awake!" and rushes to see her grandbaby. The Scripture from Zephaniah talks about God singing over us. Can you imagine God being as excited as that grandma to see you as you wake each morning?

What other images does this Scripture bring to mind?

Chapter Three

1. *"I'm sorry this has been so hard on you. It may be rough up ahead, but you know you can count on me." (p. 11)*

It is always nice to have a friend that you can depend on. Share with the group a special friend, family member, or even a pet that has been there for you in your time of need.

Chapter Four

1. *She was always drawn to the moon's radiance, whether it be as an adult when walking her dog in the evening, or as a little girl dancing in the fields under his beams. But perhaps the laughing-eyed moon's favorite recollection was Anna as a toddler with her little finger pointing towards him during story time. He was proud to have served as her*

night light. (pp. 13-14)

God has filled our skies with so many beautiful things: sunsets, rainbows, stars, the first snowfall, etc. What draws your heart? Do you recall as a child a favorite bedtime tradition, such as story time? Share a fun memory with the group.

Chapter Five

1. *A flush of shame burns up any desire in me to make future suggestions. (pp. 15-16)*

Shame and pride are the two best defensive ends that keep us from getting to our goal line. They block us from reaching out and receiving assistance. Name some other precarious team members that can hold joy at the 10-yard line.

Chapter Six

1. *Nox is acutely aware that he must get Anna to a*

secured location. (p. 17)

Nox knows that isolation is the best way to keep Anna down. By manipulating her environment, he is adding to her despair and preventing any light from shining through. What are other ways that Nox tries to control Anna?

Chapter Seven

1. *I catch myself clenching the chain, venting my frustration against the links. My fingers suddenly loosen with the realization of the hold I had on those mistakes. Nothing so cold and futile could lead to the building of a new sky. (p. 20)*

Investing our energies towards our chains in life creates more pain. It allows the circumstances in life to rob our joy. When we invest in others outside ourselves, it loosens those chains and redirects our focus. When has someone invested in your life? Share an example of how God showed you that odds don't matter, no matter how tough the circumstance, when you called on Him.

Chapter Eight

1. *He will reflect back to Anna all the goodness he sees in her, a goodness Anna had forgotten: the treasure of her soul. (p. 22)*

Nox sees Anna's broken world as useless, but Artisan sees the possibilities. For example, Nox sees the fallen pieces of sky as shards that should be discarded, while Artisan considers them gems. What other ways do Nox and Artisan's views differ as they relate to Anna's world?

Chapter Nine

1. *Whether it is a flicker or a spark, nothing's worse for Nox's plans than light. Especially a light renewed. (p. 23)*

Why would Nox find a little flicker so dangerous?

When in your life have you seen a flicker, spark, or light renewed? How have you been transformed by God's goodness and grace? Even in the midst of darkness or troubled time, how can you still have peace or joy?

Chapter Ten

1. *But feelings of inadequacy resurface as my grip loosens and is quickly followed by another misstep. Suddenly, Nox drops his portion of the chain, and I slide down the side of an amber sand dune.* (p. 26)

How quickly we slide when we start buying into negative messages about ourselves! Why are we afraid of what others may think? Are we afraid that their lack of approval means that we do not deserve to be loved? What negative images of yourself do you most struggle with?

How can we overcome these negative thoughts? Instead of focusing on winning acceptance by family, friends, or "the public," how can we turn our eyes and hearts toward the accepting embrace of Christ?

2. *The breeze kicks up, smoothing the marks of the tumble from the dune. It's wiping my slate clean! I breathe deeply. (p. 26)*

Has anyone forgiven you completely for something? Have you ever been able to forgive *yourself* completely? How does a clean slate help you move forward?

3. *I breathe slowly, trying to register what just happened. Was it the severity of Nox's guidance, his strange transformation, or this absolute darkness that scared the breath out of me? All I know is that I long for light. (p. 27)*

Depression or despair can be all-consuming. It can deceive us into believing that the current circumstance is all there is, encompassing and isolating us. How can trusting in God's guidance help us open our eyes to options? Why do we think God requires us to know the way before we take a step of faith? What Scripture passages encourage you during dark times?

4. *Minute by minute, my sense of self shrinks as the space*

I occupy seems to become too large for me. It is as if the whole world is full of spaces, with each person occupying his or her own. And how necessary is my little spot in the world when there are so many billions? If I disappear, would it really matter? Would anyone even notice? (p. 28)

Have you ever felt you are just one of many? How does God let you know that you are individually crafted for this special moment in time?

When someone spoke of Christ buying our freedom, I used to think that it was a "buy one, get one free" deal, that a soul much better than mine would be quickly ushered in to heaven, and I'd get snuck in when everybody was cheering the other guy. Yet the Bible lets us know of God's passion for each and every one of us as His precious and irreplaceable child. Do you believe you have to be valued in this world to be treasured in God's eyes? Would He have crafted ten individual fingerprints just for you if you were not a unique creation who had a story to tell and a role to play in His divine plan?

What keeps you from believing that you are in this world to pass on Christ's love to those around you?

Read Psalm 139 and name some ways it illustrates God's love and value for us.

5. *But for me it is a fortress of fears. Each moment another uncertainty enters my soul, while another bit of my freedom flies away. My eyes peek through a small opening between the feathers to see where my freedom has soared to.* (pp. 28-29)

When have you felt trapped by uncertainties? How can reaching out to God renew you and begin reconstructing a strong foundation?

6. *As a tear hits the ground, I swear no one will treat me like a failure anymore. Nox is company I will keep no longer. (p. 29)* ("Leaving Lonely," by Paul Alan ©2000 *Falling Awake,* Aluminum Records. Reproduced with permission of Paul Alan.)

I love Paul Alan's song about a girl who was changed

by a simple conversation on grace. She makes a brave choice to leave her past behind, change the unappreciated company she kept, and hold tight to Jesus, "leaving lonely behind." As Alan's song notes:

> " ... and she is determined as a tear hits the floor
> no one's going to treat her like a failure anymore
> 'cause where is the freedom in this?
> Where is the mercy in this? where's the love and respect?
> Unspeakable bliss, Where's forgive and forget?
> Where is the freedom in this?
> Yeah this is one place she's never going to miss ... "

Labels such as "failure" can stay with us a long time. It could have been from a misguided teacher to a hurting relative. In the present, we can replay those moments; hearing the word "failure" repeat in our minds. The label can sometimes not even involve a specific word but rather come from an action or lack of action someone took.

For example we could have been ignored, which causes feelings of unworthiness. Thinking we are not worthy of company we reinforce that belief which leads to isolation and loneliness.

We can even feel labeled by circumstances beyond our understanding.

A dear friend of mine decided to defy such a label. She has been battling an illness for several years. She said to me recently, "I refuse to let my illness define me." When she is up in the middle of the night with pain or going to a treatment, she repeats that mantra to herself. When the illness becomes all-consuming, she will plug into a powerful message, invest in others, or care for a rescue pet.

Those who hurt us may not have known any other way. Many times their words are coming from a place of pain. As Jesus said, "Father, forgive them, for they do not know what they are doing" (Luke 23:24 NIV). Not saying any of it was acceptable. When you realize their anger was not because of something you did or were, but because you were the nearest target, helps you let go and forgive.

The following prayer was found in the clothing of a young woman who had died of starvation in Ravensbrück Concentration Camp in northern Germany during WW II: *"O Lord ... remember not only those of goodwill ... but also those of ill will. But do not remember all the suffering they have inflicted upon us ... instead ... remember all the fruits we have borne because of this suffering ... our fellowship ... our loyalty to one another ... our humility ... our courage ... our generosity ... the greatness of heart that has grown from this trouble.*

When our persecutors come to be judged by you ... let all these fruits that we have borne be their forgiveness."

Labels trap us. They limit the vision we have for ourselves. Likewise, we may feel confined by another's limited view of our lives. Some people may only see our yesterdays. What do you say we look for and create positive relationships; those that can see/envision our tomorrows. We may have the ability to love and forgive others, but it is equally important to grow in the gift of receiving love and forgiveness from others.

How about we leave that lonely behind? Let's try some new labels. Name an adjective that describes a positive trait you've received out of difficulty. For example: you may be tenacious, innovative, a fighter, an excellent planner, determined, etc.

Chapter Eleven

1. *He crouches down to pick up his coat and begins drawing in the sand. (p. 36)*

New International Reader's Version (NIRV): "They were trying to trap Jesus with that question. They wanted to have a reason to bring charges against him." John 8:6

Just as Jesus found a way to refocus a crowd that was quick to condemn a woman for her failings, Artisan helps Anna realize that the Father's love is endless and will shower her in Living Water. When has Jesus drawn hope on the surface of your day?

2. *'The best part,"* he confides in agreement, *"is that when the storm passes, the grace remains."* (p. 40)

New International Reader's Version (NIRV): "God's gifts of grace come in many forms. Each of you has received a gift in order to serve others. You should use it faithfully." 1 Peter 4:10

What unique gift do you have that helps others? Perhaps you possess the gift of encouragement, the gift for numbers, the gift of kindness, or the gift of being a good listener, baker, organizer … Don't underestimate the gift that has been crafted in you and the power it has to help lift up others, often on a daily basis!

Create a list of gifts that you and the group possesses.

3. *"Words more numerous than these grains of sand,"* his hands sift through the tiny grains. (p. 41)

New International Reader's Version (NIRV): "If I

could count them, they would be more than the grains of sand. If I were to fall asleep counting and then wake up, you would still be there with me." Psalm 139:18

Imagine yourself relaxing on a beach, your fingers caressing the warm sand that stretches to the horizon. For each grain of sand, the Lord has a special thought about you. How uniquely precious you are to Him!

List five things that Christ might think about you. Then list ten precious thoughts you have about God! For example, He cheers for the underdog, loves children, has a sense of humor, reaches out the lonely, faithful, artistic, mighty, etc. When you are having a tough time, think about these ten neat things about the Lord. When you're done, let Him whisper to your heart some of His favorite things about you.

4. *"So next time,"* Artisan continues, *"when pressures seem too great, give them to me so that together we can make good from it."* (p. 41)

New International Reader's Version (NIRV): "We know that in all things God works for the good of those who love him. He appointed them to be saved in keeping with his purpose." Romans 8:28

Sometimes, to find hope in whatever difficult situation you are facing, it helps to look back and remember how God has helped you in the past.

A priest once told me that the Bible is like a photo album: "As you flip through the pages, it recalls all of the ways that the Lord has been faithful and has come through for you."

A blessing journal can also help with this, by taking time to note God's daily goodness. Not only will you end the day on a good note, but by reviewing God's "track record," your spirit will be renewed and help you foster a new perspective. In times of need, you can flip through this journal and be reminded of God's unfailing and passionate love for you.

Begin your blessing journal now by writing down

one way God has gifted you today.

5. *"In time, when the dark days pass, your kindness will do the same for another." (p. 42)*

Good News Translation: "The teacher of the Law answered, 'The one who was kind to him.' Jesus replied, 'You go, then, and do the same.' " Luke 10:37

When you get through a tough time, the wisdom, grace, and perspective you gain can help the next person. What a cool system! Why do you think the Lord wants us to help each other instead of going through it alone?

What lessons have you learned from going through a difficult time that you can use to help others?

6. *Taking my new friend's advice and, and before going any further, I give thanks. (p. 45)*

Good News Translation: "Be thankful in all circumstances. This is what God wants from you in your life in union with Christ Jesus." 1 Thessalonians 5:18

Anna learns to give thanks in unlikely situations by watching both the moon and Artisan. During Jesus' time on earth, He always gave thanks to His father before meals and before healing someone. A monumental time for giving thanks was when Jesus went to pray in the garden of Gethsemane. The human side of Jesus struggled with what was ahead, but He gave His Father the ultimate "thank you" by saying, "yet not my will, but Yours be done" Luke 22:39-42.

The lesson we can learn from this is that Jesus understands how we struggle to surrender our will to his. Is there anything you would like to place in His competent hands today? Ask Him to help surrender and trust in your Father as Jesus did.

Chapter Twelve

1. *Remember when we burned your cares until they became ashes and transformed into blue birds that soared*

and painted your sky? (p. 49)

New International Version (NIV): "And provide for those who grieve in Zion—to bestow on them a crown of beauty instead of ashes, the oil of joy instead of mourning, and a garment of praise instead of a spirit of despair. They will be called oaks of righteousness, a planting of the LORD for the display of his splendor." Isaiah 61:3

The Lord promises beauty for ashes. When has there been a surprise ending to your suffering?

2. *Forgiveness; the ability to absorb more pain than you inflict.*

New International Reader's Version (NIRV): "Here is the way I want you to fast. Set free those who are held by chains without any reason. Untie the ropes that hold people as slaves. Set free those who are crushed. Break every evil chain. Share your food with hungry people. Provide homeless people with a place to stay.

Give naked people clothes to wear. Provide for the needs of your own family. Then the light of my blessing will shine on you like the rising sun. I will heal you quickly. I will march out ahead of you. And my glory will follow behind you and guard you. That is because I always do what is right." Isaiah 58:6-8

To be forgiven. There's not a better feeling. Dr. Tim Keller, Senior Pastor of Redeemer Presbyterian Church in New York City shared that "forgiveness is the ability to absorb more pain than you inflict." Wow! That quote really struck me and stayed with me. I wanted to learn more so I downloaded the complete message, "And He Kissed Him." This sermon dives into the story of the Prodigal son (Luke 15:11-24).

What is the father saying? "I am not going to let you pay me back. I am not going to let you assume the debt. I am going to absorb the debt. I am going to eat it. I'm going to take the limitations and all the diminishment that comes. I'm going to absorb the debt myself."

This is the essence of what it means to forgive somebody. When someone wrongs you, they've robbed you, always. Sometimes they've robbed you of something physical and material, like money, but usually they've robbed you of something less tangible, like happiness, reputation, or opportunity. Therefore, they owe you. There's a debt. There's always a debt when someone wrongs you.

There are two things you can do with the debt: you either make them pay it back to you or you absorb it yourself. The father says, "I am going to absorb the debt." What we usually want to do when someone wrongs us is to make them pay us back. If they've hurt our reputation, then we're going to slice up their reputation to maybe get a little bit of ours back. If they've robbed us of happiness, we're going to make them unhappy to get a little bit of satisfaction back. We can make them pay, but that's not forgiveness. Forgiveness is *absorbing the debt. Therefore, forgiveness is always a form of suffering. Forgiveness is absorbing pain instead of inflicting pain.*

What portion of this message resonated with your heart most? What are some steps you can take today to make forgiveness a part of your daily routine?

Dr. Keller walks you through the other three steps to forgiveness and provides a great meter to see if you have unforgiveness in your heart. Check it out; it's not to be missed!

http://sermons2.redeemer.com/sermons/and-kissed-him

3. *Free of constraints. Theo races back into my mind, speeding down that long stretch of the lake. Completely content!* (p. 50)

Pets are a gift from God, providing comfort and friendship along with mischief and fun. What are some of your favorite ways your pets show that they are completely content?

Chapter Thirteen

1. *Artisan has destroyed his chain, link by indigo link; now another way has to be found to stop Anna, because if Artisan succeeds and restores her entire world, there will be no stopping her. She will spread Artisan's message of light to everyone. (p. 51)*

Children possess so much wonder. When they discover something, you rediscover it with them. Their smiles can make you smile. Their laughter is contagious. Have you met someone in your life whose light is so radiant that you can't help but to catch it and pass it on?

Chapter Fourteen

1. *"Take courage, Anna. Your faith has healed you." (p. 58)*

New International Version (NIV): "Jesus turned and saw her. 'Take heart, daughter,' he said, 'your faith has healed you.' And the woman was healed from that moment." Matthew 9:22

The healing touch of Jesus, incredible! When writing this book, I wanted to include a tribute to the woman who touched the hem of Jesus's garment and was healed. I love that story. I love her resilience. She had been suffering for twelve years with a bleeding disorder. This woman spent all she had to get cured but to no avail, and, because it was a bleeding disorder, the culture at that time considered her unclean. This meant people were not allowed to touch her, that she would have been separated from her family and friends, and that she could not go into the temple to worship. All that could provide comfort was denied her. Emotionally, physically, and financially exhausted, she leaned against a wall, broken.

Then Jesus comes to the town. Seeing him, she crawls through the huge crowd and reaches for his hem.

Now here is the kicker for me: "Jesus turned and *saw* her" (Matthew 9:22). For twelve years she had been treated as invisible. Now the most compassionate eyes acknowledge hers. But there's more. What does he say to her? "Take heart, *daughter*." He uses a term of endearment that instantly connected the two, and makes her a part of his family. She belonged. When I was studying youth ministry, we looked into the top ten needs of young people, and I learned that the number one need of a young person is to belong. When Jesus says, "Take heart daughter, your faith healed you," he does more than provide a medical update and encourage the woman for stepping out in faith; his love encompasses her so she is no longer an outcast but a treasured daughter. On that day Jesus did more that stop the bleeding; he healed her heart. If you feel that you are alone or have secrets you think no one will understand, turn to Jesus and listen to the special greeting he has just for you.

Where else in the Bible did Jesus do something unexpected to soften a heart and renew a soul?

Chapter Fifteen

1. *Before Artisan has a chance to speak, the lake ripples, "You are the Living Water."* [15]

> *And the clouds thunder, "You're the Good Shepherd."* [16]
>
> *The wind trumpets, "You're the Horn of salvation."* [17]
>
> *The moon beams, "You're the Light of the world."* [18]
>
> *And the sun shines, "You're the Morning Star."* [19]
>
> *The stars salute, "You're the Captain of our salvation."* [20]
>
> *And the oaks lift their branches and sway, "You're the Righteous One."* [21]
>
> *While the sunflowers bow, "You're the Seed of Abraham."* [22]
>
> *I gather my purple robe and kneel in reverence, "You're him! You're the Prince who rules over heaven and earth."* [23] *Then I lay down in thanksgiving before him, my face to the ground. (pp. 61-62)*

[15] **New American Bible:** On the last and greatest day of the feast, Jesus stood up and exclaimed, "Let

anyone who thirsts come to me and drink. Whoever believes in me, as scripture says: 'Rivers of living water' will flow from within him." John 7:37-38

[16] **New International Version (NIV):** "I am the good shepherd. The good shepherd lays down his life for the sheep. The hired hand is not the shepherd, and does not own the sheep. So when he sees the wolf coming, he abandons the sheep and runs away. Then the wolf attacks the flock and scatters them. The man runs away because he is a hired hand and cares nothing for the sheep. I am the good shepherd; and I know my sheep and my sheep know me- just as the Father knows me and I know the Father- and I lay down my life for the sheep. I have other sheep that are not of this sheep pen. I must bring them also. They too will listen to my voice; and there shall be one flock with one shepherd. The reason my Father loves me is that I lay down my life—only to take it up again. No one takes it from me, but I lay it down of my own accord. I have authority to lay it down, and authority to take it up again. This command I received from My

Father." John 10:11-18

[17] **New International Version (NIV):** "He said: 'The LORD is my rock, my fortress and my deliverer; my God is my rock, in whom I take refuge, my shield and the horn of my salvation. He is my stronghold, my refuge and my savior—from violent people, you save me. I called to the LORD, who is worthy of praise, and have been saved from my enemies.' " 2 Samuel 22: 2-4

[18] **New International Version (NIV):** "When Jesus spoke again to the people, he said, 'I am the light of the world. Whoever follows me will never walk in darkness, but will have the light of life.' " John 8:12

[19] **New International Version (NIV):** "I, Jesus, have sent my angel to give you this testimony for the churches. I am the Root and the Offspring of David, and the bright Morning Star." Revelation 22:16

[20] **New American Standard Bible:** "He said, 'No; rather I indeed come now as captain of the host of the LORD.' And Joshua fell on his face to the earth, and bowed down, and said to him, 'What has my lord to say

to his servant?' " Joshua 5:14

[21] **New International Version (NIV):** "My dear children, I write this to you so that you will not sin. But if anybody does sin, we have an advocate with the Father— Jesus Christ, the Righteous One." 1 John 2:1

[22] **King James Version:** "And deliver them who through fear of death were all their lifetime subject to bondage. For verily he took not on him the nature of angels; but he took on him the seed of Abraham. Wherefore in all things it behoved him to be made like unto his brethren, that he might be a merciful and faithful high priest in things pertaining to God, to make reconciliation for the sins of the people. For in that he himself hath suffered being tempted, he is able to succour them that are tempted." Hebrews 2:15-18

[23] **New International Version (NIV):** "For to us a child is born, to us a son is given, and the government will be on his shoulders. And he will be called Wonderful Counselor, Mighty God, Everlasting Father, Prince of Peace." Isaiah 9:6

Music has played a huge part in my faith journey. The right song at the right time, some motivating me, some challenging me, some with the car window rolled down singing at the top of my lungs and some calling me to rest quietly by his side. One of my all-time favorite tunes is "Love Song for a Savior," by Jars of Clay. In the lyrics they note, "words we can mention to show our devotion." Anna hears the universe proclaim their love for Artisan through the many names they sing out to him. What are some names you can think of to show your devotion?

Chapter Sixteen

1. *The chains, which once constricted my heart, but now have been loosened, fall to the ground. Picking up the strands, he starts to untangle them. (p. 65)*

New American Bible: "He takes away every branch in me that does not bear fruit, and everyone that does he prunes so that it bears more fruit." John 15:2

Yikes! Sometimes the pruning process can hurt! Sometimes when God is working in our lives, we can feel it. Once when praying, I told God that I was tired of making the same mistakes.

I heard in my heart, "Be patient."

Yes Lord, I said, *I will be patient as You work on these things.*

And then I felt Him gently reply, "No, be patient with yourself."

That was so freeing! God lovingly lets us grow. How can we also extend that grace and patience to others?

2. *I am afraid to share more. What's stopping you? Pride? Fear? Fear of what? Of losing control? Of sharing too much because in the past people used it against you? But it's Artisan. I'm safe with him. Maybe it's because when I say it aloud it makes it true, even though it has already happened. Or if I share my secrets with you, you'll turn away. I know you say you won't but I am still afraid. How can this part of me be loveable? (p. 68)*

New International Version (NIV): "And a leper came to Jesus, beseeching Him and falling on his knees before Him, and saying, 'If You are willing, You can make me clean.' Moved with compassion, Jesus stretched out His hand and touched him, and said to him, 'I am willing; be cleansed.' Immediately the leprosy left him and he was cleansed." Mark 1:40-42

I heard a great early morning devotional on the radio. The DJ Elle compared the leper's wounds with wounds in our soul, like bitterness, unforgiveness, addiction, and pride. Elle asked if Jesus needed to shine his light inside us and heal any of our wounds. She closed with a beautiful reminder that we can lay anything down before Jesus, whose always quick to forgive and desires to make us whole.

It's understandable that we may wince when thinking about Jesus shining his light into our hearts. There are a few things we may not want exposed. But I ran across this great verse in the Bible that says he turns everything to light: "But everything exposed by the light becomes visible, for everything that becomes visible is light" (Ephesians 5:8-14 NIRV).

Let there be light! God uses light for so many things. For example, the sun's rays helps things grow. What are some other ways light positively impacts our lives?

January 16, 2014 daily devotional reproduced with the permission of Elle Spada from WBVM Spirit FM 90.5, 717 S. Dale Mabry Hwy, Tampa, FL 33609 http://www.spiritfm905.com/

Chapter Seventeen

1. *He knows you.*

   He loves you.

   Yes, it's true.

   You are precious.

   You are treasured.

   There is more to you.

   On the good days and bad,

   his love remains the same.

   When you get up or sit down,

   he not only knows your name

but how many hairs on your precious head. [35]
He sings over you as you rise and go to bed.

Artisan turns to Anna and sings:
You are his cherished daughter,
truly one of a kind.
Your intricate carved fingerprints,
reflect this grand design.

The clouds rumble in and croon:
Nox is jealous of that love
and wants you to fail
as he weaves and winds you
down that tumultuous trail;
trying to steal your sense of self and identity,
he wants to rob you of your security.

The moon and stars back him up:
He knows you.
He loves you.
Yes, it's true.

You are precious.

You are treasured.

There is more to you.

The oak branches sway as Artisan sings:

So celebrate, Anna!

Stand tall.

You stood up to him

and spoke life into his darkness.

You are the daughter of the King.[36]

Now, you're a deeply-rooted oak,

noble and firm,

but also flexible in the breeze

to weather the many storms and torrents

knowing your father's love and inheritance

has equipped you for this moment.

My heart burns in excitement, and I start to sing:

So I'll stand tall,

I'll stand true,

I'm afraid my life, and shoulders, have been a bit

askew

under the misconception that I'm a frail flower,

but I am an oak of righteousness,

a voice needed for this hour

to hold on,

to not give up,

and to forever proclaim,

our Father's love

to all his children

again and again. (pp. 71-75)

These lyrics create the perfect lullaby for artisan and his celestial choir to sing over Anna. Think of a special little one in your life. Write several stances in tribute to that precious child. When you are finished, find an opportunity to sing it to them. Or send it to them in card. Keep those lyrics with you in your wallet. When you run across them, imagine singing it to your precious one as a daily prayer and to yourself as a reminder of how treasured you are.

Chapter Eighteen

1. *"Great." Nox paces back and forth. "She found her own voice. Unbelievable."*

"So you wanna play Artisan? Okay, let's play." Nox's right foot begins tapping and with his head shaking he warns, "You are so proud of her. You think that means that she can defend herself now. (p. 77)

The power of the human voice is amazing; to conquer darkness, encourage a soul, speak up against an injustice. Some of my favorite quotes come from people like Martin Luther King, Thurgood Marshall, Winston Churchill, and Nelson Mandela. We can also celebrate those in our own hometown like the seventh grader who stands up for a kid being bullied, the teacher or coach who inspires a young person, a mom who encourages a child who doesn't have her parent at a recital, a stranger whose complimentary words at a grocery store lifts a downtrodden soul. It doesn't have to be a major event to make a major impact. How does God want to use your voice today?

Chapter Nineteen

1. *I take the vultures as Nox's show of confidence, but it's what Artisan says that totally disarms me. "There is another thing the darkness can't stand: forgiveness." (p. 82)*

"One of my wise teachers, Dr. William F. Orr, told me, "There is only one thing evil cannot stand, and that is forgiveness." (*The World According to Mr. Rogers: Important Things to Remember* by Fred Rogers. Reproduced with the permission of Family Communications © 2003 Family Communications, Inc. Hyperion, 77 West 66th Street New York, NY 10023-6298. All rights reserved.)

I love Mr. Rogers's faith-filled message of acceptance and letting go. It's amazing how forgiveness can diffuse a situation. For some injuries, it may take some time and practice, but God can heal any wound. Share a time when forgiveness has released you.

2. *"Even for those injuries, events, sorrows, and illnesses that have occurred through no fault of your own, and that we may*

never comprehend. But in those moments, there can be a peace that passes all understanding. I'll help you carry on." (pp. 82-83)

Good News Translation: "And God's peace which is far beyond human understanding, will keep your hearts and minds safe in union with Christ Jesus." Philippians 4:7

Talk about an insurance policy! Jesus tells us that we might not understand the "why," but if we trust in the "Who," He will give us a peace to get through the "why."

What are some helpful ways that you have found to surrender those struggles and cares to God?

Chapter Twenty

1. *He laughs, then noticing a passing butterfly, nods towards it, "That's just like you, Anna." Artisan says, "The weight of her wings is technically more than she can bear. But not only does she manage to carry the weight but because of it, she dances joyfully through the air." My heart flutters with joy. (p. 86)*

The triumph of the human spirit, there is nothing like it. I often watch inspirational films, read encouraging books, and listen to positive music to keep me strong. A counselor once shared with me the story of the butterfly. What are some ways you find helpful to stay strong? Do you have a favorite story of a person or an event that rose to victory against all odds? I will never forget what one coworker shared with me over seventeen years ago, "Odds don't matter when you give it to God."

2. *And their gut instincts were right—not because of what Nox had planned for me but what you had planned for me. You knew all along that I had to die to myself, to yank out all those old weeds, so I could really be free." (p. 85)*

New American Standard Bible: "As for you, you meant evil against me, but God meant it for good in order to bring about this present result, to preserve many people alive." Genesis 50:20

New American Bible: "Even though you meant

harm to me, God meant it for good, to achieve this present end, the survival of many people." Genesis 50:20

Nox planned to end it for Anna, Artisan had other plans. Have you had a surprise ending to a tough situation? God showing up in the final seconds?

Chapter Twenty-One

1. *"Instead of allowing the darkness to overcome us, we will overcome it with light,"* Artisan explains. *(p. 88)*

New International Version (NIV): "The light shines in the darkness, and the darkness has not overcome it." John 1:5

New American Bible: "Don't let evil overcome you. Overcome evil by doing good." Romans 12:21

Self-control and I have had a tumble or two. Even when I feel like TP-ing someone's house or launching a zinger in a response to hurt feelings, I can control this—with the help of the Holy Spirit—if I remember how easily God forgives my own failings. What are some ways you can remind yourself to do good when tempted to do otherwise?

Chapter Twenty-Two

1. *"As far as the East is from the West,"* Artisan motions his right hand across the horizon, *"those things are forgotten. They are remembered no more." (p. 89)*

Good News Translation: "As far as the east is from the west, so far does he remove our sins from us." Psalm 103:12

What a freeing thought—to have your sins and faults as far away from you "as the east from the west." A passenger sitting next to me on an airplane is the one who shared the beauty of this Scripture passage with me. With the world being round, West or East is always the same distance away… an endless distance. Isn't it amazing: all of our sins are in front of Him—nothing is hidden from His sight—yet He focuses not on what we've done wrong but rather on what we are becoming and the plan He has for us!

What Scriptures can you focus on to eliminate negative self-talk and focus instead on God's grace and promises?

2. *But out of all the wonders I have seen, perhaps the most miraculous was how Artisan had created in me a new heart. (p. 90)*

New International Version (NIV): "I will give you a new heart and put a new spirit in you; I will remove from you your heart of stone and give you a heart of flesh." Ezekiel 36:26

Once when listening to the radio show, "Food for the Journey," I heard the host Sr. Anne Shields, speak about miracles. She said such a powerful thing: "People today want to see miracles like the wonders performed long ago, but perhaps, brothers and sisters, the most miraculous miracle of all, is how He [God] touches and changes each one of our hearts.

("Food for the Journey" can be accessed through *renewalministries.net*. Reproduced with permission by

Sr. Ann Shields, S.G.L.)

How have you seen God touch and change your heart?

In 1 Kings 19:12 the writer explains that the people were waiting to hear from God. And God being GOD, they thought He would communicate in a BIG way—in flashes of lighting or the roar of the sea—but the author explains God's language of love is often much more intimate. "After the earthquake came a fire, but the Lord was not in the fire. And after the fire came a gentle whisper."

Sometimes we are afraid to be still. Afraid of what God wants to share with us. We are afraid of what we might hear, or worse that we may not hear Him at all. I encourage you to be still. If you find that difficult, ask God to help you. Perhaps focusing on one word can help, such as "peace" or "love" or listen to your heart beat.

God loves you so much and has so many wonderful things He wants to share with you! He is waiting to whisper those words of love, but like any good friend, He waits until you invite him in.

3. *"I am with you always." he reminds me. (p. 90)*

New International Reader's Version (NIRV): "Teach them to obey everything I have commanded you. And you can be sure that I am always with you, to the very end." Matthew 28:20

You never walk alone. Call on Him and He is there by your side before the words leave your lips. Spend a quiet moment in prayer, thanking God for always being with you.

4. *He exhales and breathes his spirit upon me. (p. 90)*

New International Reader's Version (NIRV): "I will ask the Father. And he will give you another Friend to help you and be with you forever." John 14:16

Unsure which way to go? Jesus promised that He would send us a friend, a helper to get us through. Call on the Holy Spirit to provide guidance, to be your own personal home team, to root you on to the finish line with wisdom and love.

How can you remind yourself to call upon the Holy

Spirit throughout the day?

5. *He smiles. "The Spirit will teach you what you need to know, bringing forth kindness, goodness, faithfulness, humility, and strength of will to your world." (p. 91)*

Good News Translation: "But the Spirit produces love, joy, peace, patience, kindness, goodness, faithfulness humility and self-control." Galatians 5:22-23

Wow! All that good stuff comes with the Holy Spirit! And that's not all ... if you act right now, you will also get the loving Father and His life-changing Son ... call today!

As you journey through life, Christ lovingly cultivates these fruits in you to bless others. Which of these fruits have not yet ripened in your life? Why?

Which fruits have ripened to the point that friends and coworkers have noticed? Stay away from false humility here; bear witness to what God has done for you!

6. *"Remember to guard your heart; it is the wellspring of*

life." *(p. 91)*

New American Bible: "With all vigilance guard your heart, for in it are the sources of life." Proverbs 4:23

New International Reader's Version (NIRV): "Above everything else, guard your heart. It is where your life comes from." Proverbs 4:23

Good News Translation: "Be careful how you think; your life is shaped by your thoughts." Proverbs 4:23

It's really easy to get distracted, with all the media and messages coming your way. Just like whatever you put in your body affects you one way or another, so does your daily intake of TV, music, office gossip, and celebrity misbehavior.

You have the power to choose what you let into your life by the things you read, the television you watch, the websites you visit, and the gossip you pass along.

What change can you make in your habits to free yourself from the constant and distracting social chatter?

7. *"For where your heart is, that is where your treasure will also be."* (p. 91)

New American Bible "For where your treasure is, there also will your heart be." Matthew 6:21

It's funny how easily my heart can be distracted. It quickens both at the possibility of working on a project that is a dream of mine and buying a new bright and shiny thing that I absolutely do not need!

If I focus my heart on treasures outside of the Lord, I seem to always keep wanting, running, and craving. When I focus on Him, I feel well-nourished and my desire for "things" fades. When I spend more time with the Lord, my hunger pangs for things are less.

What false treasures distract you?

When Artisan uses the word "treasure," what does he mean?

8. *"Most importantly, know that nothing can separate you from my love."* (p. 91)

New American Bible: For I am convinced that neither death, nor life, nor angels, nor principalities, nor present things, **nor future things, nor powers,** nor height, nor depth, nor any other creature will be able to separate us from the love of God in Christ Jesus our Lord. Romans 8:38-39

New International Reader's Version (NIRV): I am absolutely sure that not even death or life can separate us from God's love. Not even angels or demons, the present or the future, or any powers can do that. Not even the highest places or the lowest, or anything else in all creation can do that. Nothing at all can ever separate us from God's love because of what Christ Jesus our Lord has done. Romans 8:38-39

Good News Translation: "For I am certain that nothing can separate us from his love: neither death nor life, neither angels nor other heavenly rulers or powers, neither the present nor the future, neither the world above nor the world below—there is nothing in all creation that will ever be able to separate us from the love of God which is ours through Christ Jesus our Lord." Romans 8:38-39

Nothing can separate us from God's love—and I

mean N-O-T-H-I-N-G. If you hadn't had the chance, chat with Him today about something you feel is separating you from Him. He knows all, but like a good friend, he enjoys hearing your take on things! Just check out Jesus' track record in the mercy department; in the Gospel, nothing separated Him from folks that came to Him.

Discuss examples from the Bible of Jesus' mercy.

9. *Looking into his eyes, I know that is true because with Artisan, anything is possible. (p. 91)*

New International Reader's Version (NIRV): "Jesus looked at them and said, 'With man, that is impossible. But with God, all things are possible.' " Mark 10:27

New American Bible: Jesus looked at them and said, "For human beings it is impossible, but not for God. All things are possible for God." Mark 10:27

Good News: "Jesus looked straight at them and answered, 'That is impossible for human beings but not for God; everything is possible for God.' " Mark 10:27

Pretty much sums it up. ☺

Additional Discussion Questions:

Artisan rebuilds Anna's world. He lights her path and provides simple truths that ease her burdens and protect her for the journey ahead.

When I recall Jesus saying, "I am the way and the truth and the life" (John 14:6), I think of *The Wizard of Oz* film. Remember when Dorothy is beginning her journey and the Munchkins tell her to "Follow the yellow brick road?" With each step on the brick road, the path lights up and she moves closer to her goal.

What happens when she steps off the road to snack on some fruit? She gets pelted with apples by a disgruntled tree. There is safety and protection in God's guidelines, not because He is bossy, but because He wants us to stay safe. Just like a loving parent, He will provide discipline—a word that means teaching, not spanking—when needed so we grow into adult Christians. The Lord loves when we are child-like but not child*ish*.

How have God's guidelines saved you? What behaviors or thoughts is He calling you to discard or add, as you mature?

Take-home Encouragement for Discussion Groups:

Leader: Please feel free to print the following quote on cards and pass them out to the participants at the end of the book discussion.

People are like stained-glass windows; they sparkle and shine when the sun is out, but when the darkness sets in, their true beauty is revealed only if there is a light within.

~ **Elizabeth Kubler-Ross**

Notes

1. **NIRV:** "The Lord your God is with you. He is mighty enough to save you. He will take great delight in you. The quietness of his love will calm you down. He will sing with joy because of you." Zephaniah 3:17

2. Inspired from the song, "Leaving Lonely," by Paul Alan ©2000 *Falling Awake*, Aluminum Records. All rights reserved used by permission of Paul Alan.

3. **NIRV:** "They were trying to trap Jesus with that question. They wanted to have a reason to bring charges against him." John 8:6

4. **NIRV:** "God's gifts of grace come in many forms. Each of you has received a gift in order to serve others. You should use it faithfully."1 Peter 4:10

5. **NIRV:** "If I could count them, they would be more than the grains of sand. If I were to fall asleep counting and then wake up, you would still be there with me." Psalm 139:18

6. **NIRV**: "We know that in all things God works for the good of those who love him. He appointed them to be saved in keeping with his purpose." Romans 8:28

7. **Good News:** "The teacher of the Law answered, 'The one who was kind to him.' Jesus replied, 'You go, then, and do the same.' " Luke 10:37

8. **Good News:** "be thankful in all circumstances. This is what God wants from you in your life in union with Christ Jesus.1Thessalonians 5:18

9. **NIRV:** "Here is the way I want you to fast. Set free those who are held by chains without any reason. Untie the ropes that

hold people as slaves. Set free those who are crushed. Break every evil chain. Share your food with hungry people. Provide homeless people with a place to stay. Give naked people clothes to wear. Provide for the needs of your own family. Then the light of my blessing will shine on you like the rising sun. I will heal you quickly. I will march out ahead of you. And my glory will follow behind you and guard you. That is because I always do what is right." Isaiah 58: 6-8

10. **Good News:** "Love is patient. Love is kind. It does not want what belongs to others. It does not brag. It is not proud. It is not rude. It does not look out for its own interests. It does not easily become angry. It does not keep track of other people's wrongs.

Love is not happy with evil. But it is full of joy when the truth is spoken. It always protects. It always trusts. It always hopes. It never gives up." Corinthians 13:4-7

11. **NIV:** "Jesus turned and saw her. 'Take heart, daughter,' he said, 'your faith has healed you.' And the woman was healed

from that moment." Matthew 9:22

Good News: "Jesus turned around and saw her, and said, "Courage, my daughter! Your faith has made you well." At that very moment the woman became well. Matthew 9:22

12. **NIV:** "For you were once darkness, but now you are light in the Lord. Live as children of light (for the fruit of the light consists in all goodness, righteousness and truth) and find out what pleases the Lord. Have nothing to do with the fruitless deeds of darkness, but rather expose them. It is shameful even to mention what the disobedient do in secret. But everything exposed by the light becomes visible—and everything that is illuminated becomes a light." Ephesians 5: 8-13

13. **NIV:** "Be strong and courageous. Do not be afraid or terrified because of them, for the LORD your God goes with you; he will never leave you nor forsake you." Deuteronomy 31:6

14. **NIV:** "And now these three remain faith, hope, love. But the greatest of these is love." 1Corinthians 13:13

15. **NAB:** On the last and greatest day of the feast, Jesus stood up and exclaimed, "Let anyone who thirsts come to me and drink. Whoever believes in me, as scripture says: 'Rivers of living water' will flow from within him." John 7:37-38

16. **NIV:** "I am the good shepherd. The good shepherd lays down his life for the sheep. The hired hand is not the shepherd, and does not own the sheep. So when he sees the wolf coming, he abandons the sheep and runs away. Then the wolf attacks the flock and scatters them. The man runs away because he is a hired hand and cares nothing for the sheep. I am the good shepherd; and I know my sheep and my sheep know me- just as the Father knows me and I know the Father- and I lay down my life for the sheep. I have other sheep that are not of this sheep pen. I must bring them also. They too will listen to my voice; and there shall be one flock with one shepherd. The reason my Father loves me is that I lay down my life—only to take it up again. No one takes it from me, but I lay it down of my own accord. I have authority to lay it down, and authority to take it up again. This command I received from My Father." John 10:11-18

17. **NIV:** "He said: 'The LORD is my rock, my fortress and my

deliverer; my God is my rock, in whom I take refuge, my shield and the horn of my salvation. He is my stronghold, my refuge and my savior—from violent people, you save me. I called to the LORD, who is worthy of praise, and have been saved from my enemies.' " 2 Samuel 22: 2-4

18. **NIV:** "When Jesus spoke again to the people, he said, 'I am the light of the world. Whoever follows me will never walk in darkness, but will have the light of life.' " John 8:12

19. **NIV:** "I, Jesus, have sent my angel to give you this testimony for the churches. I am the Root and the Offspring of David, and the bright Morning Star." Revelation 22:16

20. **NASB:** "He said, 'No; rather I indeed come now *as* captain of the host of the LORD.' And Joshua fell on his face to the earth, and bowed down, and said to him, 'What has my lord to say to his servant?' " Joshua 5:14

21. **NIV:** "My dear children, I write this to you so that you will not sin. But if anybody does sin, we have an advocate with the Father—Jesus Christ, the Righteous One." 1 John 2:1

22. **KJV:** "And deliver them who through fear of death were all their lifetime subject to bondage. For verily he took not on him the nature of angels; but he took on him the seed of Abraham. Wherefore in all things it behoved him to be made like unto his brethren, that he might be a merciful and faithful high priest in things pertaining to God, to make reconciliation for the sins of the people. For in that he himself hath suffered being tempted, he is able to succour them that are tempted." Hebrews 2:15-18

23. **NIV:** "For to us a child is born, to us a son is given, and the government will be on his shoulders. And he will be called Wonderful Counselor, Mighty God, Everlasting Father, Prince of Peace." Isaiah 9:6

24. **NIV:** "What do you think? If a man owns a hundred sheep, and one of them wanders away, will he not leave the ninety-nine on the hills and go to look for the one that wandered off? And if he finds it, truly I tell you, he is happier about that one sheep more than the ninety-nine that did not wander off. In the same way you Father in heaven is not willing that any of

these little ones should perish." Matthew 18:11-14

25. **NAB:** For my yoke is easy, and my burden light." Come to me all who are tired and are carrying heavy loads. I will give you rest. Become my servants and learn from me. I am gentle and free of pride. You will find rest for your souls. Serving me is easy, and my load is light." Matthew 11:28-30

26. **NIV:** "The Lord is my shepherd, I lack nothing. He makes me lie down in green pastures, he leads me beside quiet waters, he refreshes my soul. He guides me along the right paths for his name's sake. Even though I walk through the darkest valley, I will fear no evil, for you are with me; your rod and your staff, they comfort me. You prepare a table before me in the presence of my enemies. You anoint my head with oil; my cup overflows. Surely your goodness and love will follow me all the days of my life, and I will dwell in the house of the Lord forever." Psalm 23

27. **Good News:** "Let the wicked leave their way of life and change their way of thinking. Let them turn to the Lord, our God; he is merciful and quick to forgive." Isaiah 55:7

28. **NAB:** "For sin is not to have any power over you, since you are not under the law but under grace." Romans 6:14

29. **NAB:** "and you will know the truth, and the truth will set you free." John 8:32

30. **NIV:** "Come near to God and he will come near to you." James 4:8

31. **NAB:** "For I am convinced that neither death, nor life, nor angels, nor principalities, nor present things, nor future things, nor powers, nor height, nor depth, nor any other creature will be able to separate us from the love of God in Christ Jesus our Lord. Romans 8:38-39

32. **NIV:** "For I am confident of this, that he who began a good work in you will carry it on to completion until the day of Christ Jesus." Philippians 1:6

33. **NAB:** "For you did not receive a spirit of slavery to fall back into fear, but you received a spirit of adoption, through which we cry, "Abba, Father!" Roman 8:15

34. **NIV:** "You know when I sit and when I rise; you perceive my thoughts from afar." Psalm 139:2

35. **NIV:** "What I tell you in the dark, speak in the daylight; what is whispered in your ear, proclaim from the roofs. Do not be afraid of those who kill the body but cannot kill the soul. Rather be afraid of the one who can destroy both soul and body in hell. Are not two sparrows sold for a penny? Yet not one of them will fall to the ground outside your Father's care. And yet the very hairs of your head are all numbered. So do not be afraid; you are worth more than many sparrows." Matthew 10:27-31

36. **NAB:** "For God is king over all the earth; sing hymns of praise." Psalm 47:8
NIV: "For God is the King of all the earth; sing praises with a psalm of praise." Psalm 47:7
NAB: "For you did not receive a spirit of slavery to fall back into fear, but you received a spirit of adoption, through which we cry, "Abba, Father!" Roman 8:15

37. Create and send us your own song to Anna via poetry, music

art, etc. and share it with us at www.cooperandrogers.com.

38. **NIV:** "Jesus said, 'Father, forgive them, for they do not know what they are doing.' " Luke 23:34

39. **NASB:** You have taken account of my wanderings; Put my tears in Your bottle. Are they not in Your book? Psalm 56:8

40. **NIV:** "You will again have compassion on us; you will tread our sins underfoot and hurl our iniquities into the depth of the sea." Micah 7:19

41. **NAB:** "For God is king over all the earth; sing hymns of praise." Psalm 47:8
NIV: "For God is the King of all the earth; sing praises with a psalm of praise." Psalm 47:7
NAB: "For you did not receive a spirit of slavery to fall back into fear, but you received a spirit of adoption, through which we cry, "Abba, Father!" Roman 8:15
42. **NIV:** "Since you are precious and honored in my sight, and because I love you, I will give people in exchange for you, nations in exchange for your life." Isaiah 43:4

43. **NIV:** "For I know the plans I have for you,' declares the LORD, 'plans to prosper you and not to harm you, plans to give you hope and a future.' " Jeremiah 29:11

44. **NIV:** "You are my hiding place; you will protect me from trouble and surround me with songs of deliverance." Psalm 32:7

45. "One of my wise teachers, Dr. William F. Orr, told me, 'There is only one thing evil cannot stand and that is forgiveness.' " *The World According to Mr. Rogers: Important Things to Remember* by Fred Rogers. Reproduced with the permission of Family Communications © 2003 Family Communications, Inc. Hyperion, 77 West 66th Street New York, NY 10023-6298. All rights reserved.

46. **Good News:** "And God's peace which is far beyond human understanding, will keep your hearts and minds safe in union with Christ Jesus." Philippians 4:7

47. **NIV:** "You yourselves are our letter, written on our hearts, known and read by everyone. You show that you are a letter from Christ, the result of our ministry, written not with ink but with the Spirit of the living God, not on tablets of stone but on tablets of human hearts." 2 Corinthians 3:2-3

48. **NIV:** "The light shines in the darkness, and the darkness has not overcome it." John 1:5

49. **Good News:** "As far as the east is from the west, so far does he remove our sins from us." Psalm 103:12

50. **NIV:** "I will give you a new heart and put a new spirit in you; I will remove from you your heart of stone and give you a heart of flesh." Ezekiel 36:26

51. **NIRV:** "Teach them to obey everything I have commanded you. And you can be sure that I am always with you, to the very end." Matthew 28:20

52. **NIRV:** "I will ask the Father. And he will give you another

Friend to help you and be with you forever." John 14:16

53. **Good News:** "But the Spirit produces love, joy, peace, patience, kindness, goodness, faithfulness humility and self control." Galatians 5:22-23

54. **NAB:** "With all vigilance guard your heart, for in it are the sources of life." Proverbs 4:23
NIRV: "Above everything else, guard your heart. It is where your life comes from." Proverbs 4:23
Good News: "Be careful how you think; your life is shaped by your thoughts." Proverbs 4:23

55. **NAB:** "For where your treasure is, there also will your heart be." Matthew 6:21

56. **NAB:** For I am convinced that neither death, nor life, nor angels, nor principalities, nor present things, **nor future things, nor powers,** nor height, nor depth, **nor any other creature will** be able to separate us from the love of God in Christ Jesus our Lord. Romans 8:38-39

NIRV: I am absolutely sure that not even death or life can separate us from God's love. Not even angels or demons, the present or the future, or any powers can do that. [39] Not even the highest places or the lowest, or anything else in all creation can do that. Nothing at all can ever separate us from God's love because of what Christ Jesus our Lord has done. Romans 8:38-39

Good News: "For I am certain that nothing can separate us from his love: neither death nor life, neither angels nor other heavenly rulers or powers, neither the present nor the future, [39] neither the world above nor the world below—there is nothing in all creation that will ever be able to separate us from the love of God which is ours through Christ Jesus our Lord." Romans 8:38-39

57. **NIRV:** "Jesus looked at them and said, 'With man, that is impossible. But with God, all things are possible.' " Mark 10:27

NAB: Jesus looked at them and said, "For human beings it is impossible, but not for God. All things are possible for God." Mark 10:27

Good News: "Jesus looked straight at them and answered, 'That is impossible for human beings but not for God; everything is possible for God.' " Mark 10:27

The Scripture references come from the following:

Scriptures and additional materials quoted are from the Good News Bible © 1994 published by the Bible Societies/ HarperCollins Publishers Ltd UK, Good News Bible© American Bible Society 1966, 1971, 1976, 1992. Used with permission.

Scripture texts in this work are taken from the New American Bible, revised edition © 2010, 1991, 1986, 1970 Confraternity of Christian Doctrine, Washington, D.C. and are used by permission of the copyright owner. All Rights Reserved. No part of the New American Bible may be reproduced in any form without permission in writing from the copyright owner.

Scripture texts in this work are taken from the HOLY BIBLE, NEW INTERNATIONAL VERSION & NEW INTERNATIONAL READER'S VERSION Holy Bible, New International Version®, NIV® Copyright © 1973, 1978, 1984,

Acknowledgements

*T*he *Stained Glass Heart*, the book that love built. Thank you to all who have accompanied, prayed, encouraged, read, shared, re-read, and journeyed with me over the past eight years while I completed this story.

To Darcy Nickel, Sean Gannon, Julie Terrwilliger, and Chris and Anne Treston for being there in the early days and continuing your support throughout the years.

To Heidi Allwood and Christi McGuire for their assistance in conducting the book discussion groups. Special thanks to Heidi for all of her research and marketing suggestions and to Christi (www.ChristiMcGuire.com) for her excellent help in editing the book.

Additional proofreaders who were always there to take time review the manuscript and share their insights: Caitlyn Nicole Durfee, Gail Somodi, Megan Pritchard, Patti Ann Papiano, Pam Eubanks, Kelly Pleasant, Cristy Lopez, Emily Mingote, and Robert Collier.

Marie Gruber, for her assistance and perspective with the use of pastels for the book cover. Patti Ann Papiano, for her assistance during my retreat in being the first to read the additional seven chapters.

To all the women who have participated in the book discussion groups throughout the years.

Thank you to the youth who participated in the feedback sessions, including: Amanda Denise Durfee, Sierra Beeson-Rolle, Nathalie Kabango, Caroline Krupa, Vincent Franco, Tara Barg, Ashley Hills, and Kiely Huhyn.

To the following for the encouragement, guidance, wisdom, love, and support:

Viola Cooper, Bernice Frierson and family, Christy Lopez, Fawn Germer, Nory Napan, Linda Christenson, Kristin Michel Rodriguez, Suzanne Torroni, Heather Reece, Allison Kummery, Pastor Berkley Helmes, Pastor Jim Freeman, Laura Freeman, Ineta McPartland, Deacon Ron Dains and Sylvia Dains, Mary Heider, Adriana Florez, Marcie Ahlistrand, Jim Donahue, Sandi Donahue, Sarah Donahue, Anna Paula Marquez, Cindy Perkins, Shannon Beeson-Rolle, Maryanne McCarthy, Janet Rogers, Janet and Bill Friend, Debbie Becker, Julie Katchen, Margaret Fenner, Kathleen Durfee, Mary Jo Flaherty-Keller, Bill Flaherty, Melinda Mullin, Robin Hughes, Adriana Rushing, Robyn Zeyher-Morgan, Pat Martino, Eliana Rodriguez, Todd Williams, Lawrence Williams, Denise Little,

Steve Laube, Christin Ditchfield, Chris Culp, Neirda LaFontant, Valerie Funk, Greg Funk, John Henry Bourke, the McNulty family, Klara Mascitto, Anne Jennison, Joshua, Lynne Gillard, Diane Flaherty, Carolyn and Phil Babas, Daisy and Angie Vulvovich, Sr. Teresa Benedicta, Marina Kolbe Hutchinson, Pam Brown, CeCe Pritchard, Rita Affeld, Anna Sandberg, Bob Keeshan, Dorothy Klodnicki, Debbie Jackson, Kate Bradford, Louise White, Michelle Helwege, Fatima Turay-Conteh, Esther Conteh, Emmie and David Walsh, Sally Schoeffel, Liz Cashen, Tina Weger, Monica Mingote, Diane Warmus, Stephen Treston, Charlie, Tim Walsh, Pat & Fritz Gregoire, Lori Augustyniak, Lance, Sam, William Wu, Mary Jane and Ed Souza, Bev Latine, Julie Corbett, Sherry Stipsky Dion, Joe, Mary, Joan, Lucy, Rita, Vimal Kunwar, Barbara Leis, Lori Tucker, Sandy Thomas, Melissa Williams, the Hills Family, Mark and Maricile O'Brien from Rocket Digital, Margie and Sharon from Hope Haven's Children's Hospital.

To my neighbors and friends, coworkers and classmates, in LA, DC, Chicago, Detroit, Wilmington, Bradenton, Dayton, Jacksonville, and Sarasota, in thanksgiving for making all of those places my home.

To all my wonderful teachers and tutors, those who have helped me in academics and in my spiritual life, I am very grateful.

To my treasured nieces and nephews, Thomas, Megan, Kate, Mandy, Will, Hannah, and Alex, I love you bunches.

To all that I have gotten to know through fostering pups, I am grateful for you and to be a part of your loving families. To all the rescue groups and humane societies, vets and volunteers, for your tireless efforts, love, and care to homeless pets.

Theo wishes to thank: Gus, Maggie, Orion, Luna (aka Eden), Little Mo, Mr. Blue, Mina, Yeti, Smoochies (aka Maggie), and all the Wee Beans. He also wants to thank Gunner, Carmen, Quincy, Dixie, Mason, Monty, Pixie, Lily, Marley, Mikey and Gracie.

To the Youth Pastors, Youth Ministers I've worked with and those who I've fellowshipped with in the Out East Breakfast Group, Pastor Berkley Helmes, Father Kevin in Ireland, Father Carl Birarelli, Father Damian, Father Jerry O'Mahony, Father Dan, Joyce Meyer, Les Brown, Pope John Paul XXIII, Pope Francis, Father Dan Cody, Father Tom Cody, Father Dan Logan, and Tenth Avenue North's Video Devotionals.

For the colorful inspiration: Agnes F. Northrop, Tiffany Studio (New York), Smith Museum of Stained Glass Windows, Navy Pier, Chicago, IL, and The Charles Hosmer Morse Museum of American Art.

For all the folks of different denominations and faith who have shared with me the love of God.

Thank you illustrators Caitlyn Nicole Durfee and Ariana Raquel for the incredible chapter art icons. I love your soulful interpretations of the story.

To the families that I have served as a babysitter or nanny and those special children: Juno, Gemma, Dylan, and Claire.

A special shout out to all the members of the Our Lady of the Angels Youth Group and the youth lectors—you have made my life so rich.

In appreciation for all source materials cited in *The Stained Glass Heart* Book:

Dr. Tim Keller, Senior Pastor of Redeemer Presbyterian Church, New York City, NY; Andi Brindley, Clara Lee, Redeemer City to City, Fred Rogers and Family Communications, Sister Ann Shields of Renewal Ministries, Elle Spada Spirit FM 90.5 Tampa, FL, Elizabeth Kubler-Ross, Globe Communications Group, American Media Inc., Songwriters, Paul Alan, to Deacon Rick Zandy for introducing me to the Ravenstock prayer during his homily on forgiveness.

Thanks also to Growing Interactive US for enhancing

Chapter 12 with the opportunity to learn more about effective weeding and the opportunity to include the below paraphrased sentence from their video "Easy Weeding - How to Get Rid of Weeds in Your Vegetable Garden," Reproduced with the permission of Growing Interactive LLC© 2013 by http://www.growveg.com:

"Did you ever hear that old adage 'one year of seeding means seven years of weeding?' It means that the seeds of the weeds can remain in the soil for years and when matured those weeds rob the plants of their nutrients, light, air and water, preventing them from growing."

All Bible translations including: Good News Bibles, the Bible Societies/HarperCollins Publishers Ltd UK, American Bible Society, New American Bible, Confraternity of Christian Doctrine, Washington, D.C., New International Version & New International Reader's Version, Zondervan Publishing House, *The New American Standard Bible, The Lockman Foundation, and King James Version.*

In thanksgiving for all the creative activities and prayers cited in *The Stained Glass Heart* Retreat:

"The SunFlower" Centering Prayer: Judi Gaitens, St. Andrew the Apostle Roman Catholic Church, Apex, NC. Administrative assistance by Ann Marie DiSerafino, St. Andrew the Apostle Roman Catholic Church, Apex, NC

"Planting Sunflower Seeds": Cristy Lopez

"Around the Oak Tree": Prayer Paul Jasmer, OSB with administrative assistance provided by Susan Sink of Episcopal House of Prayer, Collegeville, MN

"Tumbleweed or Tree": Nancy Ruegg, http://nancyaruegg.com/2014/05/05/tumbleweed-or-tree/

"Tissue Stained Glass Heart Craft": Wee Folk Art, Reproduced with the permission of Wee Folk Art (copyright 2010) www.weefolkart.com, weefolkart@yahoo.com

"Alcohol Ink Stained Glass craft project": Patti Ann Papiano, Cristy Lopez, and Adriana Florez

This book is a thank-you note back to you, Jesus, for being the light in my story.

About the Author

Maureen Ann Flaherty (aka "Mo") is a writer, public speaker, marketing consultant, actor, and doggie foster mom. She has worked in corporate communications, for non-profit groups, and held some interesting jobs, such as acting the lead role in an Emmy-nominated short film, *Radioman* and operating a forklift.

Her first book, *The Portable Sister*, was published by Andrews McMeel. The little encouragement book is like having a sister to cheer you on throughout the day.

Mo describes herself as an "idea person" and splits her time between working in youth ministry and writing books with her collaborator and best friend, Theo, her black lab.

"When you get in a tight place
and everything goes against you,
till it seems you could not hold on a minute longer,
never give up then,
for that is just the place and time
that the tide will turn."

~ **Harriet Beecher Stowe**

Credits

Front Cover: Maureen Ann Flaherty, image inspired by Autumn Landscape (1890's) designed by Agnes F. Northrop and fabricated at Tiffany Studio (New York). Smith Museum of Stained Glass Windows, Navy Pier, Chicago, IL

Back Cover: Maureen Ann Flaherty

Chapter Icons: illustrated by Caitlyn Nicole Durfee and Ariana Raquel

Book Designer: Barb Willard, www.basicdezigns.com

CPSIA information can be obtained
at www.ICGtesting.com
Printed in the USA
FFOW05n0351251014